Counseling
and
Divorce

RESOURCES FOR
CHRISTIAN COUNSELING

RESOURCES FOR CHRISTIAN COUNSELING

VOLUME EIGHTEEN

Counseling
and
Divorce

DAVID A. THOMPSON

RESOURCES FOR
CHRISTIAN COUNSELING

—————— General Editor ——————

Gary R. Collins, Ph.D.

WORD PUBLISHING
Dallas·London·Vancouver·Melbourne

An effort has been made to locate sources and obtain permission where necessary for the quotations used in this book. In the event of any unintentional omission, modifications will gladly be incorporated in future editions. Permission to quote from the following sources is gratefully acknowledged:

An adaptation of "Family Promises" by Craig Dykstra, from Faith and Families, copyright 1986, The Geneva Press.

Remarriage and God's Renewing Grace by Dwight Hervey Small, published by Baker Book House, 1986.

Recovery from Divorce by David A. Thompson, published by Bethany House Publishers, 1982.

The Seasons of a Man's Life by Daniel J. Levinson, published by Alfred A. Knopf, 1978.

Mere Christianity by C. S. Lewis, published by Macmillan, 1958.

Rebuilding: When Your Relationship Ends by Bruce Fisher, published by Impact Publishers, 1981.

Marriage, Divorce, and Remarriage in the Bible by Jay E. Adams, published by Zondervan, 1980.

Whatever Happened to Commitment? by Edward R. Dayton, published by Zondervan, 1984.

Jesus and Divorce by William A. Heth and Gordon J. Wenham, published by Thomas Nelson, 1984.

Married People: Staying Together in an Age of Divorce by Francine Klagsbrun, © 1985 by Francine Klagsbrun, published by Bantam Books.

Caring and Commitment by Lewis B. Smedes, © 1988 by Lewis B. Smedes. Published by Harper and Row.

Library of Congress Cataloging-in-Publication Data

Thompson, David A.
    Counseling and divorce / by David A. Thompson.
       p.   cm. — (Resources for Christian counseling ; v. 18)
    Bibliography: p.
    Includes index.
    ISBN 0-8499-0496-X
    1. Divorce—Religious aspects—Christianity. 2. Marriage counseling. 3. Pastoral counseling. I. Title. II. Series.
BV4012.27.T48 1988   88-27249
253.5—dc19   CIP

Printed in the United States of America

1 2 3 9 AGF 9 8 7 6 5 4 3 2

CONTENTS

EDITOR'S PREFACE

Several years ago my parents celebrated their fiftieth wedding anniversary. Their picture appeared in the newspaper, they got messages of congratulations from the mayor and from the Prime Minister of Canada, the family had a dinner party, and friends came to offer best wishes. Watching the events of that weekend, I was surprised at the number of times I heard someone state that it was a "remarkable achievement" for any couple to stay together for half a century.

Some people, of course, don't live that long; but for many couples it is the marriage that fails to survive. The reasons may be numerous, complex, and unique to each situation. Even so, many marriages crumble and disintegrate long before anyone thinks about a golden anniversary.

The prophet Malachi wrote that the Lord hates divorce (Malachi 2:16)—but so, I suspect, do most of the people who experience the lingering pain and trauma of a marriage breakup. Jesus recognized that some marriages would not survive, despite the initial good intentions of both husband and wife. The divorce rate in our society has skyrocketed and often our best counseling efforts fail to prevent the breaking up that leads to so many broken lives.

In this book, David Thompson writes about the breaking up and the broken lives. With compassion, sensitivity, biblical awareness, and the experienced perspective of a seasoned counselor, he describes how we can help people who are divorcing, divorced, or watching others cope with the end of a marriage. The author writes from the perspective of a pastor, professional counselor, and former navy chaplain who has seen many couples struggle with divorce.

Several years ago, Dave wrote a workbook designed to help couples and individuals recover from divorce. At the time he asked me to write a foreword which could apply equally well to the book that you hold in your hands. "David Thompson has spent many hours with men and women who are going through the pain of divorce," I wrote. "He has seen their discouragements, struggles and feelings of failure—and he has been able to help them move toward hope and recovery. This book does not defend or condone divorce, or take a light view of marriage. The author has a high view of marriage coupled with a deep sensitivity for those whose marriages have failed."

Like all of the volumes in the Resources for Christian Counseling series, this book is intended to be practical and helpful. Written by counseling experts, each of whom has a strong Christian commitment and extensive counseling experience, the books in this series are meant to be examples of accurate psychology and careful use of Scripture. Each is intended to have a clear evangelical perspective, careful documentation, a strong practical orientation, and freedom from the sweeping statements and undocumented rhetoric that sometimes characterize writing in the counseling field. Our goal is to provide books that are clearly written, useful, up-to-date overviews of the issues faced by contemporary Christian counselors. All of the Resources for Christian Counseling books have similar bindings and together they are intended to comprise a helpful encyclopedia of Christian counseling.

For ten years, David Thompson was a chaplain in the United States Navy. One of his last assignments was service at a Navy-Marine Corps Family Service Center on Okinawa. There, he handled all of the marriages, saw over one hundred people for premarital counseling every month, cofacilitated spouse-abuse treatment programs, and conducted divorce-recovery groups. In part because of dedication to his own marriage and family, he resigned from the navy and is now professor of practical theology and counseling at Bethany College in Minnesota. In response to some gentle persuasion on my part, he agreed to turn aside briefly from his doctoral dissertation to write this book.

Probably this is the only book in the series that was written, in part, on a U.S. Navy ship rolling through heavy seas in waters off the Pacific coast! But this is the work of a man who has both feet planted firmly on solid theological and psychological ground. I hope you find it helpful as you gently lead divorced and divorcing people toward needed healing, divine forgiveness, personal growth, and new beginnings.

Gary R. Collins, Ph.D.
Kildeer, Illinois

Counseling
and
Divorce

RESOURCES FOR
CHRISTIAN COUNSELING

INTRODUCTION

WHY IS IT SO HARD TO SAY "GOOD-BYE"?

Saying "good-bye" is never easy! In my years in ministry, I have seen more than my share of people saying "good-bye." First, as a hospital chaplain, I watched terminally ill patients bid families farewell when death was imminent. I said good-bye to my mother this way.

Then, as a navy chaplain, I saw loved ones embrace at an airport or on a pier, as navy personnel departed for lengthy service on a ship or at an overseas base. I hugged my wife and sons and said good-bye this way.

Finally, as a pastoral counselor, I have seen couples end their marriages with a lot of sadness and bitterness. This is a harsh and hurtful way to say good-bye. Although I have never separated from my loved ones in this way, I have stood at "the wake" for many marriages that have died.

It is painful to see people part. Divorce, like death, is grief at its worst! In times like these, caregivers wish they could "make it all better." But many times we can't!

I can remember a particularly hectic day several years ago. I had seen five couples in counseling, with four adamantly refusing to even try to repair their marriages. The fifth couple, by far the most hopeless, said they thought they could "work things out" without my help. I left my office feeling frustrated and discouraged because I had lost several more couples to the Big "D" (Divorce). I think I must have grieved over the loss of those couples to divorce much like an oncologist grieves over the loss of patients to cancer. As the physician despises death, so I despised divorce. Yet I eventually realized my hatred of divorce was directed at the wrong target. Divorce was not the *cause* of the problem. The real enemy was sin.

This book is written by a pastor and Christian counselor for other pastors and Christian counselors. I make no apology for being promarriage. Yet, I am aware that sometimes marriages suffer disease and some of them die. So this book has been written to help pastors and other counselors understand some of the dynamics of divorce. I have outlined some intervention strategies which may be useful in attempting to salvage a troubled marriage. But ultimately, this book deals with a Christian response to the divorced and the divorcing. My desire is that it will help you provide counsel that cares.

This book is written in appreciation of the hundreds of couples whom I have counseled, who have struggled with the pain of divorce. Their honesty and openness provided insights for me into the divorce process which has made this book possible. Hopefully, through their sacrifice, healing and wholeness may be possible for many others. A special note of thanks goes to Gary Collins, editor, mentor, and friend, who encouraged me in my interest in the integration of theology and psychology. I would like to express my appreciation to Terry McDowell, friend and colleague, for many hours of hard work preparing this manuscript for publication. Also, my love and gratitude is given to Judy, my bride of eighteen years, for her encouragement and editorial assistance in this project.

CHAPTER ONE

THE CAUSES OF DIVORCE

HAVE WE LOST OUR CHRISTIAN MIND-SET?

As a boy in rural northern Wisconsin, I watched numerous auto accidents occur near my home. The two-lane blacktop road nearby had a sharp curve which had to be negotiated with great care, especially at night or in stormy weather. Frequently, I would hear the sirens of sheriffs' cars and ambulances and see their flashing lights as they arrived at that corner. I would jump on my bike and ride toward the accident to get a better look. Often I'd observe how the authorities handled the victims of these accidents. Usually a sheriff's deputy arrived on the scene first, setting flares to warn other motorists of the danger. He and the ambulance crew ran to the wrecked vehicle to check for injured passengers. Sometimes

13

they had to put out fires or pry people from the wreckage before giving life-saving first aid.

Only after all of that was done did the police officers begin to interview drivers, passengers, or other witnesses; only then did they measure skid marks to help them determine what caused the mishap. And only after they had thoroughly investigated the accident did they begin to assess blame or guilt. The police didn't ticket drivers until they found conclusive evidence of negligence or wrongdoing. The investigators had to decide: Should judgments be made which would result in road repair or more noticeable warning signs? Or should citations be issued for human error, law violations, or negligence?

When drivers were fortunate enough to walk away from these accidents, often I could overhear their explanations for the mishaps: "I wasn't warned about the sharp curve." "My brakes locked." "The road was slick with rain." "Maybe I was driving a little too fast." I sometimes guessed these drivers had been intoxicated or at least had been careless or inattentive.

Thinking back to these accidents, I now attribute them to one of three causes: 1) willful disobedience of known laws, 2) inattention to mechanical problems or changing road conditions, or 3) unpredictable events beyond the driver's control. Maybe an oncoming car was driven by a drunk or reckless driver; maybe a sudden cloudburst, a freak patch of ice, an unmarked pothole, or debris in the road caused the crash.

When we look at the problem of divorce, often a more devastating event than a traffic accident, we approach it with the same priorities of a good police officer at the scene of an accident. Primary concern must first be to minister to the needs of the injured, and to prevent others, as much as we can, from experiencing the same kind of devastation. Only when this emergency aid has been given should we begin searching for causes of the break-up and make judgments and decisions that we hope will reduce the number of future divorces.

Too often, however, the Christian community has approached such accidents with premature judgments and insensitive neglect of the hurting. Rather than quickly rescuing the injured from the wreck, the church has allowed the victims to suffer while it measures skid marks ("whose fault is this?") and takes testimony from witnesses ("who's heard the latest rumors?"). We seem to want to assign blame, pass judgment, and deliver punishment for offenders. Such behavior, at best, reveals a misguided sense of priorities; at worst, it is spiritual negligence. That is not to say assessments should never be made; but our greater concern should be for the spiritual and emotional recovery of our people.

As pastors and counselors, it is vital that our motives and attitudes be Christlike when we intervene in catastrophic situations. A pastor or counselor can act like a police officer who views each accident as a reflection on his or her inability to enforce the law, resenting every accident-prone driver who would spoil the district's safe-driving statistics. Likewise, some pastors view divorces within their congregations as an embarrassment to them and their community. It somehow says their ministry to many couples has been ineffective.

A pastor's first response may be to ignore the problem, hoping it will go away. The second response often is frustration. Then Christian leaders may use God's law to try to force people to obey their marriage vows: "God does not approve of divorce." Instead of dealing with this lawbreaking as a symptom of deep spiritual and emotional problems, many pastors make superficial attempts to simply stop the divorce: "Everyone has marriage conflicts. You can work yours out if you really try."

The problem is that such measures only partially prevent divorce by scaring some people into staying married. This remedy doesn't address the emotional or spiritual issues which cause the self-destructive behavior. So the marital discord and covenant breaking continue, perhaps more discreetly. Or problems are driven underground only to manifest themselves in other negative ways. Spouse or child abuse, illicit sexual affairs, overeating, excessive drinking, and workaholism are some of the ways these unresolved conflicts reveal themselves.

How do we effectively minister to the divorced and the divorcing in a genuinely caring manner while remaining faithful to the Word of God? While they deal with the immediate pain of separation, empathic helpers will also begin searching for the causes of the problems. Counselors will recognize the external pressures our society places on couples and families. Too often, pastors and counselors ignore contextual issues in assessing marriage conflicts. They immediately delve into spiritual or psychological problems without assessing systemic and historical issues that may have led to a particular behavior. Genuine help comes from the pastor or counselor who shows compassionate concern and who makes an assessment involving three areas: environmental issues, interpersonal conflicts, and psychological problems.

ENVIRONMENTAL ISSUES

First, let's look at environmental issues which place tremendous stress upon American families and Christian couples in particular. Charles Swindoll, in his book *Come Before Winter and Share My Hope,* reminds us of the mind-boggling changes that have taken place in our society:

> Less than a hundred years ago the Sunday sermon was the chief occasion of community instruction . . . the *only* time for formal instruction of *any* kind. The Bible was the nucleus of shaping minds and determining decisions. What a difference today! . . . We are the target of a deadly accurate dense-pack of information: an endless number and variety of books, media persuasion, and secular propaganda with its appealing influences flying at us at the speed of light.
> Our thinking is changing.
> Truth is now up for grabs.[1]

The philosophical impact of existential ethics and relative values has spread throughout American society. Humanists would tell us there are no absolute ways to live. Right and wrong are totally in the eye of the beholder. Professor Allan Bloom at the University of Chicago, commenting on a cross section of student life, states, "There is one thing a professor can be absolutely certain of: Almost every student entering the university believes that truth is relative."[2] Such an outlook means a loss of an organizing spiritual principle by which to live. This irreligious state creates a vacuum. Bloom says:

The dreariness of the family's spiritual landscape passes belief. It is as monochrome and unrelated to those who pass through it as are the barren steppes frequented by nomads who take their mere subsistence and move on. The delicate fabric of the civilization into which successive generations are woven has unraveled, and children are raised, not educated. . . . I am speaking here not of the unhappy, broken homes that are such a prominent part of American life, but the relatively happy ones, where husband and wife had nothing to give their children in the way of a vision of the world, of high models of action or profound sense of connection with others.[3]

Where prior generations may have faced a road paved smooth with absolute values, the frost of relativism has caused that road to buckle and become filled with potholes for today's travelers.

Even in Christian homes, doctrinal thinking has been affected by this absence of absolute truth. The authority and reliability of Scripture, as a guide for twentieth century living, is ignored or rejected. As a pastor, I am constantly confronted with parishioners who are illiterate biblically and ethically. When social/ethical issues such as divorce or abortion are discussed, I quickly discover our lack of common ground. My attempt to counsel can easily become an exchange of opinions and situational ethics with no historical or biblical basis. As long as counselees recognize no authority other than my own human position and wisdom, my opinions can be readily argued and such discussions quickly dismissed.

Many couples' ideals and goals for life have dramatically shifted; they started out with a Christian consensus and have drifted into a secular mind-set. What used to be a great calling to "Love God with all your heart and your neighbor as yourself" has been perverted to "Love yourself with all your heart and let your neighbor watch out for himself." Self-sacrifice has given way to self-fulfillment and brotherly love has turned into self-love. Servanthood has been abandoned for success and financial security. Individuality and autonomy are praised, while community and responsibility are viewed as anachronisms.

Couples are usually not aware how dramatically their environment has changed, and how subtly their own thinking has conformed to this new age.

Pastors sense this schizophrenia in the lives of couples who attend their churches and seek their counsel. Even evangelical Christians sometimes have great difficulty integrating their Monday-through-Saturday lives with their Sunday faith. When Christians are called to live according to God's standards in human relationships, valuing honesty, sexual purity, justice, and humility, it sounds so right—on Sunday. Yet, on Monday morning, from the first glance at the morning paper, to the push and shove of the world of school and work, the world shouts at them: "Look out for Number One!" "Do your own thing!" "You only go around once in life—so go for the gusto!" Advertising repeatedly and blatantly declares that popularity, sexual attractiveness, and status are primary goals. These same Sunday churchgoers are told throughout the week that happiness can be found in a Hawaiian vacation, a lake home, or a powerful executive position.

Interspersed in this bombardment of powerful propaganda is a pragmatic throwaway mentality which discourages long-range commitments of any kind. On Sunday, the goal of sacrifice is preached; on Monday the goal is success. On Sunday, holiness is our aim; on Monday, it's happiness. There is a maddening dichotomy between the two worlds, often resulting in hypocrisy and incongruent behavior in both spheres. Perhaps it was this dichotomy Christ described when he commanded us to be in the world, but not of the world.

It is all too common to hear of the church deacon who cheats on his taxes, is unethical in his business, and is viciously competitive among co-workers. Nor is it entirely surprising to hear of his wife's becoming dependent on alcohol or drugs or getting involved in an affair with someone more attentive to her needs.

More often, however, the Christian family is caught up in a more socially acceptable, bland version of materialism and existentialism. They mix skewed values with tepid religious beliefs and end up with an anemic faith.

This kind of compartmentalized living is illustrated by a story told to me by a Christian submarine commander. He was invited to a party with other commanding officers of U.S. ships in the Philippines. To his horror he discovered it was being held in an establishment known for acts of sexual exhibitionism. Quickly he began to make his apologies and find an exit from the place. Before he could leave, the proprietor grasped him by the arm and invited him to stay. Backing out into the street, he said to the woman, "I am a Christian, and, because of that, I can't stay here."

Her face lit up and she declared: "But, I'm a Christian, too! I graduated from an evangelical Bible school near Manila, and I love the Lord!" With a puzzled look on his face, the naval officer asked, "How can you be in such a business and call yourself a Christian?"

She answered, "That's easy. This is my business and that (pointing off to a church in the distance) is my faith."

Ed Dayton, of World Vision International, writes about such an attitude in his book, *What Ever Happened to Commitment?*: "We isolate what we believe from what we do; we divide fact from all responsibility for those facts; and we are left with 'truth without consequences.'"[4]

Just because people have become members of the church or given testimony of faith in Christ, they or their marriages are not necessarily exemplary as Christian. In fact, many pastors and counselors are confronted with Christian couples whose faith is peripheral, at best, to what is really important in their lives. Dayton describes such living this way:

> Seeing ourselves as playing different roles allows us to avoid becoming Christians at the core of life. Rather than seeing our Christian life as fundamental to every other part of life, too often we see it as just another role we play. . . .
>
> Instead of seeing all of life as part of Kingdom life, our citizenship is a part-time affair. We are very much like citizens of one country who hold passports to another: They have potential citizenship in two countries. Many of us need to burn one of our passports and make a lifetime commitment to a group of fellow citizens.[5]

How did their Christian faith become so nonessential? Like the victims of the auto accidents described earlier, many

Christian couples are experiencing the consequences of "inattentive driving" in their world. They feel the anxiety of having missed some turns, finding themselves far from where they started spiritually, yet not quite sure that they want to go back. No one can live schizophrenically for very long without being forced to make some choices. Jesus describes this dilemma when he commands us to choose between God and mammon, loving one and hating the other (Matt. 6:24). The only other alternative is to slowly go insane, trying to live a double life.

People come to Christian counselors seeking relief from conflict-filled relationships. They are willing to participate in marriage-enrichment programs, communication skills classes, and behavior modification for specific, self-defeating habits. Yet, for many, at root is an inner life with conflicting loyalties between Christian beliefs and an existential and materialistic environment that has deeply corroded and corrupted much of their thinking. Short of a dynamic conversion to Jesus Christ, nothing will ever be placed in proper order. Value conflicts can only be resolved by making value choices. An individual must accept one Lord of life while he or she rejects the other. That is both good theology as well as good psychology.

INTERPERSONAL CONFLICTS

Many couples approach Christian marriage and family life with unrealistic expectations. The title of Charles Dickens's classic *Great Expectations* could be used as the title of the book many brides and bridegrooms would write about marriage. Much of this is fostered by a romantic, rather than Christian, understanding of love. The love portrayed in the media implies that another person can meet all of one's needs and complement all one's areas of inadequacy.

No one but God himself is capable of meeting all our needs. If one or both partners persist in holding on to such ideas, they soon become disillusioned with their spouse's inability to care for them. Such idealistic thinking will rob the relationship of its joy and plant the seeds for marital failure.

My wife and I received as a wedding gift a recording featuring Louis H. Evans, Jr. speaking on Christian marriage. He spoke of several ingredients in a good marriage but named two that are essential: The ability to accept each other as we are, offering liberal doses of forgiveness for each other's idiosyncrasies, and a commitment to something bigger than ourselves, namely the Lord himself. His advice addressed realistically the human condition and the divine provision. This advice has guarded us from a form of idolatry which could have ruined our marriage.

Most couples repeat traditional wedding vows expecting much more of the "better" than the "worse." Very few would risk their entire future on a venture they believe is bound for disaster. And, so, selectively, they hear the minister intone "for better . . . for richer . . . in joy . . . in health," as they screen out negative phrases like "for worse . . . for poorer . . . in sorrow."

We somehow expect life to treat us kindly. According to James Dobson,

> We feel almost entitled, by divine decree, to at least 72 years of bliss, and anything less than that is a cause for great agitation. In other words, our level of expectation is incredibly high. But life rarely delivers on that promise. It deals us disappointment and frustration and disease and pain and loneliness, even in the best of circumstances.[6]

Difficulties do come: A spouse struggles with vocational or financial failure; illness strikes; accidents happen; a spouse or child becomes alcohol or drug dependent; or in-laws cause recurring problems. Most of us may have hoped for fairness and even perhaps a reward for our righteous living; yet to expect that in a sin-darkened world is folly. The record of Scripture reveals numerous examples of pain to be endured as we wait for the deliverance which is to come. "Therefore we do not lose heart. Though outwardly we are wasting away, yet inwardly we are being renewed day by day. For our light and momentary troubles are achieving for us an eternal glory that far outweighs them all" (2 Cor. 3:16–17).

It is when the expectations of sunny days are met with the realities of storms that our relationship is tested. Those who can accept such trials and adjust their expectations to the demands of reality survive to enjoy better days, while others fail for their lack of flexibility and endurance.

We do have the choice of shaking our fist at the world, whining, "It isn't fair!" How often counselors hear the words, "If only this hadn't happened." As the children's rhyme declares, "If ifs and buts were candy and nuts, every day would be Christmas." Short of heaven, we will experience less than the ideal in life.

Many sincere individuals enter marriage believing good marriages are conflict-free marriages. Where there are differences, many partners want to remake their mate in their own image. Such remodeling projects are doomed to failure! In reality, a certain degree of conflict is normal between people with different histories, personalities, and communication styles. Someone once quipped if two partners agree on everything, one is totally redundant and unnecessary!

Salvador Minuchin, psychiatrist and therapist, believes conflict is an integral part of married life: "The TV view of families presents a distorted idea—that people need to be free from conflict. . . . Actually, every family has conflict—not only families who seek therapy. Marriages are essentially exercises in conflict."[7]

Francine Klagsbrun, in her book *Married People: Staying Together in the Age of Divorce,* talks of marriage as a process open to change rather than as an inflexible ideal which cannot adapt to upsetting circumstances:

> Marriage is a process because it always is in flux; it never stays the same and never completes itself. It is a process of changing and accepting changes, of settling differences and living with differences that will never be settled; of drawing close and pulling apart and drawing close again. Because it is a process that demands discipline and responsibility, it can bring frustration and pain, but it can also plumb the depths of love and provide an arena for self-actualization as nothing else can.[8]

Klagsbrun notes that, "Those who remain married and satisfied with their marriages are willing to discard their fantasies and build a richer and deeper life beyond the illusion."[9]

Probably many couples need to pray the Alcoholics Anonymous prayer in regard to their marriages: "God grant me the strength to change the things I can change, the ability to accept the things I cannot change, and the wisdom to know the difference."

Many misunderstandings arise because couples are not clear as to what they mean when they say, "I love you." For many it means, "I like you; your personality, appearance, sexuality, or sense of humor is attractive to me." But then the love lasts only as long as the other person maintains these qualities. The problem is that many of these characteristics won't stand up well over time; they will sparkle or fade with changing circumstances. Consequently, a person can be falling in or out of love with each seasonal change in the spouse's life.

Christian marriage, on the other hand, views love as an intentional act: I covenant with my mate to live sacrificially for her or for him. The apostle Paul, in 1 Corinthians 13, spells out what love is:

> Love is patient, love is kind. It does not envy, it does not boast, it is not proud. It is not rude, it is not self-seeking, it is not easily angered, it keeps no record of wrongs. Love does not delight in evil but rejoices with the truth. It always protects, always trusts, always hopes, always perseveres. Love never fails! (vv. 4–8).

What is noteworthy is that Paul speaks in behavioristic terminology, listing observable behaviors, not vague feelings. Paul goes on to declare, in Ephesians 5:21–33, that mutual submission marks the Christian marriage. As Christ lived sacrificially for the church to sanctify it, so also Christians in marriage should live for one another. Such loving action toward one's spouse ultimately becomes the highest form of loving and valuing of oneself. Christian love wants to give before there is a promise of receiving. It is a commitment to be there for someone else— to be for them and their best interests, even when others may abandon them. "Commitment is at the foundation of all human relationships. . . . We are made to live in relationship with others. The person who withdraws all commitment to others ceases to be human."[10]

23

Commitment to love another person is a sign of spiritual and emotional maturity. To embark upon marriage with any expectation other than to "grow up" spiritually and emotionally is unreasonable.

PSYCHOLOGICAL PROBLEMS

Many divorces are caused by psychological problems in one or both partners. Numerous individuals come to marriage with a clouded past. They have grown up in homes where family violence, sexual abuse, and alcoholism were a part of life. These people can suffer from low self-esteem and an inability to give or receive love because of such environments.

Depression and anger fill many lives. Fiancées can conceal such negative traits during courtship, only to have them erupt destructively after the wedding. The spouse was viewed as the one who could save the individual from some horrible environment or abusive situation. The problem is the partner from a violent home brings a lot of "baggage" to the marriage. Perhaps none of us fully realizes the lasting effects of such a history.

Even Christian couples come together with differing levels of understanding and commitment to the Christian faith. At face value, their oneness of faith would seem to be a great unifier. But couples' different understandings of law and grace, God's sovereignty and man's freedom, and the extent and effects of sin upon man affect the way marriage partners order their lives. Guilt and anger caused by legalistic upbringing emerge again and again in the counselor's office. Couples struggle with their understanding of God, his Word, and the Christian community. Questions of God's presence and power trouble many individuals, and they cry out at crisis points, "Where are you, God? Why don't you act to deliver me?"

As Os Guinness writes in his book, *In Two Minds,* many people struggle with a mental picture of an all-powerful but angry God, or an all-loving but impotent God. Guinness expresses people's view of God as: "I know you could if you would, but you probably won't . . . [or] as, I know you would if you could, but you probably can't."[11] If couples live with such distorted pictures of spiritual reality, significant conflict can evolve in their relationships.

Combine this with conflicting views of gender roles a couple will play, as husband/wife, father/mother, provider/nurturer, and a marriage can quickly become chaotic. Most of us learn these roles as children, through observation of our own parents. If our models were positive and loving, we bring some rich images into our marriages to guide us in our own behavior. If, on the other hand, the models were angry and competitive, we will have poor information to guide us in fulfilling these roles ourselves.

Many psychological needs for self-esteem are played out in an inordinate and unbalanced pursuit of money, sex, and power. Though it is the external environment that offers these temptations, the frenzied pursuit after them is internal. Many times counselors hear clients say, "If only I could have a hundred thousand dollars . . ." or "If I could just get that regional manager's position with its power and perks . . ." or "If I could only have a relationship with a caring and exciting person . . . then I would be happy!" Obviously, all of this externalizing doesn't deal with the internal forces that are causing the empty feelings. And so we see people flitting from place to place, job to job, and person to person, hoping to put together an unrealistic combination of great geography, soul-satisfying work, and deeply fulfilling relationships. They fail to look inwardly at their own undernourished spirits.

Couples who come to us are, in reality, asking for a drastic change of scenery through divorce. The counselor or pastor has a wonderful opportunity to help these clients to first look within themselves before reordering their external world.

A word needs to be said regarding partners who suffer violence and cruelty at the hands of their mates. Joanne was one such wife who came to me for counseling. Tom's only job was playing guitar in a hard-rock group. He would come home high on drugs about 3 A.M. (after the bar where he performed closed), and want to get his wife and two preschoolers out of bed to party with him. If they were sleepy or reluctant in any way, he would get angry and punch them. This abuse had gone on for several weeks when Joanne came, bruised and puffy-eyed, asking if it was ever all right for a Christian to leave a partner.

Many spouses go out of their way to accommodate, compromise, and appease such a partner, often uselessly. Some divorces take place simply because it is too dangerous for the spouse or children to remain with such abusers, particularly if they refuse to seek treatment.

Spouses who leave this kind of marriage might live with a lot of guilt, constantly second-guessing their action: "If only I had stayed, maybe I could have helped my spouse." For those people, divorce is but a funeral for a marriage already murdered by psychological or physical abuse.

The same could be said for the partner who is abandoned by an unfaithful spouse. The one who is left may experience a deep sense of regret and failure. Counseling may reveal the disintegration of the marriage commitment long before "divorce" was ever mentioned.

In review, I believe that an anti-family environment, interpersonal conflicts, immaturity, and psychological problems may all contribute to the crashing end of a marriage. Counselors may also point to the lack of a sense of community to support couples when problems are small and still manageable. Not so many years ago, concerns were shared over a cup of coffee or over the backyard fence with neighbors. Families who move every three or four years don't develop that kind of close relationship with neighbors. Extended families may live a thousand miles or farther away. As a result, all the emotional support a husband or wife receives is from the spouse. But, in our highly competitive, fast-paced society, one or both spouses may come home from work too drained of energy to even listen.

I am convinced the root cause of divorce is a spiritual crisis. William E. Hulme, author of *The Pastoral Care of Families*, agrees: "Marital problems are often simply old problems with a new environmental setting. They are problems in relating to oneself, others, and God that often antedate the marriage."[12] Men and women are isolated from each other by a deadness in their own spirits. A husband or wife looks externally for answers that can only be found in a human spirit made alive by God's Spirit.

When we look at the causes of divorce, we conclude that some of these accidental deaths of marriages could be prevented. Pastors and other Christian leaders should recognize warning signs and make timely interventions. There is probably a time for all couples, who have even a spark of love left for each other, when that love can be fanned back to life. However, when the devastation of divorce does occur, we need to respond in such a way that our people survive the crash and receive the kind of treatment which will lead to healing and wholeness again.

Jason Towner takes his readers through his own months of separation and divorce in *Jason Loves Jane, But They Got a Divorce.* This is the way he describes his own woundedness:

> I know what it is like to come home to an empty house, my mate gone. I know what it is to receive "greetings" from a court clerk. I know what it is to eat alone, to sleep alone, to be alone. I know about TV dinners, housecleaning, and overdue bills. I know what it means to be sexually frustrated, malnourished, misunderstood, and angry—to be a nonfunctioning adult. I know what it means to blame, doubt, fear, accuse, regret.[13]

We, as Christians, are commanded to bind up the bruised and broken, and surely that includes the divorced and divorcing.

CHAPTER TWO

THE CRISIS OF DIVORCE

WHAT MAKES SIN A BARGAIN?

Several years ago I sat in a class in Marriage and Family Counseling and heard a professor ask, "What makes sin a bargain?" What makes it such a good deal to side with evil rather than good? What unfulfilled desires are so urgent that they overpower people, causing them to justify immoral shortcuts? In psychological jargon, what is the "payoff" for aberrant behavior?

The professor believed that once you have the answer to that question, you have a clue to the treatment program that brings healing and wholeness. In short, it becomes a "bargain" to get well psychologically. In theological terms, the pursuit of righteousness becomes more attractive than the bent toward sin.

Certainly, the problem of evil is not totally explained in behavioristic terms (i.e., actions don't fully reveal the total personality); however, it is a starting point to begin looking at the issue of human failure, particularly as it applies to divorce.

The apostle Paul tells us in Romans 3:23, "All have sinned and fall short of the glory of God." Sin is not only *with* us but *in* us. We all have endorsed it and embraced it. No matter how much we legislate against sin, the temptation to engage in destructive and hurtful behavior doggedly follows us throughout life. Greed, pride, hatred, jealousy, lying, slander, stealing, murder, and sexual immorality are all prolific in our world. We marvel that goodness and righteousness survive at all in this hostile environment. By all appearances, sin is on sale at rock-bottom prices; there is no similar bargain on holiness.

Divorce, which concludes the sin of covenant-breaking, is just one of a whole catalog of actions that fall short of the divine plan for our lives. God's standard could hardly be more clearly stated: "I hate divorce, says the Lord God of Israel" (Mal. 2:16). Jesus qualified this decree in Matthew 19:8–9, acknowledging that in certain cases (specifically adultery/unfaithfulness) divorce was the lesser of two evils.[1] The apostle Paul, in writing to the Corinthian church, encourages unequally yoked couples to stay married as long as the non-Christian desires to remain in the marriage.[2] This leaves abandonment and adultery, according to Jesus' teaching, as the only exceptions that permit divorce.[3]

Divorce was clearly not God's intention, for it was his plan from the beginning for man and woman to remain faithful throughout life.[4] It was the breaking of that covenant which makes divorce so loathsome to God. Divorce is like a "funeral" for a dead marriage that was killed by unthinking neglect or unfaithfulness to "the wife of your marriage covenant."[5]

Each year, divorces are taking place in disheartening numbers. There were 2.4 million marriages and 1.16 million divorces in the United States in 1986.[6] That trend, somewhat down from the seventies, has remained fairly constant over the past decade in the United States. Within the church, divorce is on the rise among Christian entertainers, clergy couples, and laity.[7] Marriage enrichment programs flourish and bookstore shelves have become filled with self-help books on marriage.

Yet marriages continue to fail, proving that information alone is not the solution. No amount of peer pressure nor religious prohibitions seems to stem the tide of divorce. What can Christian counselors and pastors do to address this issue in their communities? What makes sin a bargain from psychological and theological perspectives?

PSYCHOLOGICAL PERSPECTIVES

The comedian Flip Wilson used to quip in his routine, after a wicked joke, "The devil made me do it." Yet, making choices for good or evil is more complex than that. The apostle James declares, "Each one is tempted when, by his own evil desire, he is dragged away and enticed. Then, after desire has conceived, it gives birth to sin, and sin when it is full grown, gives birth to death" (James 1:14–15 NIV).

If we are concerned about the sin of covenant breaking, which leads to divorce, we need to ask ourselves, "What makes people vulnerable to walking away from God's explicit will for their lives?" Obviously, this question does not just apply to divorce, but to a whole range of sinful behaviors. Why do people break promises, lie, cheat, commit adultery, get involved in alcohol or drug addiction, or sell their souls to the pursuit of power and possessions? What makes it such a good deal to do these things? Is righteous, healthy living so boring that it is unrealistic? Is it possible to create an environment or community where it is a bargain to be righteous?

Several years ago when one of my sons was a kindergartener, he got into a habit of lying after household accidents. His mother and I would hear something crash in the living room, and we would run to find a broken vase or knickknack. We would ask him what happened, and he would usually answer, "I dunno."

Finally, one day my son and I were playing catch in the backyard, and I asked him, in an unguarded moment, why he was lying to us after all these incidents. He looked at the ground and explained quite simply, "Because I don't like spankings!" After thinking about his answer, I promised him, "I will never spank you *except* for lying!" (I figured I could find some other appropriate discipline for other kinds of disobedience.)

From that day on, it became a good deal to be honest, and his behavior changed markedly. That doesn't mean there never were relapses—or never any more spankings (old sinful habits die hard), but there was genuine progress toward honest confession of wrongdoing by my son.

The point I am trying to make here relates to the issue of divorce and the church. The problem we faced in our home was *our* problem, not just my son's problem. How easy it is to make *scapegoats* of the offenders when we play a part in their negative behavior. My son, in his natural inquisitiveness to explore and investigate new things despite our prohibitions, reached out for the vase. This was combined with his lack of knowledge of the fragile nature of porcelain and glass objects, or lack of appreciation for their value to us. He was still very immature, exercising bad judgment and poor eye-hand coordination in handling such delicate objects. In short, an accident was waiting to happen.

We, his parents, on the other hand, assumed a level of maturity that wasn't there. Occupied with other things, we did not properly supervise our son's activities. We foolishly allowed the living room to get disturbingly quiet with a youngster in the room, while my wife and I chatted about really "important things" in another room. When a figurine crashed to the floor, we rushed in with disappointment on our faces and anger in our voices and asked, "What happened?" or "Who did this?" Being the smart boy that he was, he quickly assessed, by previous painfully memorable experience, that honesty would not be rewarded. He began to point fingers at his brothers, or he vaguely replied, "I dunno." Only when we made it safe to be honest did this behavior change.

We need to acknowledge at the outset that divorce is *our* problem, not just the problem of those divorcing. We, as a church, have been busy about so many important things—building programs, budgets, outreach committees—that we have neglected the couples and families to whom we're ministering. They, meanwhile, have been adopting humanistic ideas and trying worldly activities, with limited maturity and experience. We have assumed that people who attend our church or are Christians, have truly Christian mind-sets and Christian marriages. That may be far from reality! I suspect many couples are just going through the motions. They're living with just "a form of godliness." The church, like parents, expects the ideal. When, in fact, the marriage crashes like the figurine, we feel angry, hurt, and betrayed by someone we thought we could trust.

Our judgmental reactions will often lead to a defensiveness and justification of wrongdoing by the offenders; it does not lead to repentance, forgiveness, and restoration. We then react to this lack of repentance with further criticism, and a cycle of recrimination and ostracism continues. Like Captain Bly, we try to flog sailors until their morale improves!

And it's not only those who are judged for their wrongdoing who are affected. Onlookers to this process resolve to "desert ship" if they get in a similar situation. So, instead of our correcting one bad situation with criticism and punishment, that situation only becomes worse, with other couples' similar problems being driven below the surface.

As a church, we want to monitor the spiritual development and nurturing of our people. This may involve cell groups or other means by which intimacy can be developed. Douglas A. Anderson, in his book *New Approaches to Family Pastoral Care*, describes one such method of getting into people's lives:

A former seminary professor of mine, Dr. Gerhard Frost, told me recently of a colleague's experience when visiting Africa. He drove over a hill at dusk and saw ahead a series of fires stretching across the plain. As he drove near he discovered that each fire was a campfire in the center of a village. Around the fire gathered all the tribe's families, telling and retelling the stories of the tribe. Dr. Frost concluded, "This is a good model for the church—the community of the story."

Anderson goes on to say,

I want to encourage churches to gather their families around campfires and fireplaces to share their stories. In such rich, late-night sharings families can learn from others how they have gotten through a life cycle passage, and families can nourish and strengthen each other for the journey.[8]

Sensitive leaders can intervene before sinful behavior becomes habitual and destructive. Where discipline is required, it is done in the context of a supportive community. Small groups allow for correction and education without the residual bitterness, anger, and fear which may come from a more public and humiliating approach to problems.

J. Carl Laney, in his book *A Guide to Church Discipline,* seems to call for this kind of sensitivity when he says, "Because church discipline is designed to be corrective rather than punitive, the sinner's situation, spiritual sensitivity, and state of repentance must be considered as church discipline is exercised."[9]

Counselors have often viewed aberrant and destructive actions as symptoms of deeper issues in people's lives. Sin is rarely mentioned in counseling books, but most Christian helpers would agree that underlying sin, inherited predispositions, and past experiences can all influence our actions.

The first reaction of a counselor when clients begin to describe their problems with lying, cheating, sexual immorality, or jealousy is to accept people right where they are. The goal of the counselor's interviewing approach is to help clients change their troublesome behavior, often through this process of insight.

When a client comes to a counselor and says, "I'm thinking about getting a divorce," usually the counselor is neither visibly shocked nor judgmental. The counselor is interested in the environmental conditions, relational conflicts, or psychological needs that drive a person to take such a drastic step. All counseling from then on is aimed at helping a client deal with those needs and make wise decisions. For Christian counselors, of course, this includes relating a couple's decisions and actions to their faith in God and to the teaching of Scripture.

In contrast, pastors have more often viewed abnormal behavior as sin, a violation of the known will of God. Their primary orientation by training and philosophy is to make value judgments and give advice about behavior and attitudes. They base their counsel primarily upon Scripture or theology and secondarily upon contemporary Christian cultural norms. Three observations about pastoral counseling are worth noting.

First, the pastor's training emphasizes a prophetic model that wholeheartedly seeks to retard evil in society and to stand for goodness and righteousness. Pastors sense a responsibility to uphold institutional values and ideals of the Christian faith. They often use the confrontive style of the prophet as a model for ministry.

Second, if one's theology envisions the church as a people living separated from the world and striving for purity, it is hard to accept moral failure among the membership. In some circles, there seems to be a belief that there is an instant immunity from sin and temptation among believers upon their conversion. There is little appreciation for the drastic effects of the Fall on mankind.

Third, a pastor's focus is not just on the individual, but also on the group. Most ministers feel torn between institutional concerns for a holy, sanctified church and the needs of individual church members who are failing to measure up to the ideal.

When many couples come to pastors, contemplating divorce, the pastor's conflicting roles (steward of the institution as well as a shepherd of the sheep) get in the way of total concern for the individual. The couple is admonished to work harder at their marriage. (This reinforces the assumption by many people that the only counsel an evangelical pastor will give is to reconcile.) Most often, the couple will feel the pastor doesn't know how hard they've already tried to make their marriage a success—or at least to avoid divorce. The result is the couple quickly terminates counseling and often leaves the church as well. Obviously, pastors want to be more helpful in their counseling.

THEOLOGICAL PERSPECTIVES

Pastors need some new patterns for ministry in addition to the prophetic model. We recall Jesus himself in his dealing with both the Samaritan woman and Zacchaeus (see John 4:4–42 and Luke 19:1–10). It is noteworthy throughout Jesus' ministry that he sought out sinners and frequented their homes so often that he was highly criticized by the religious leaders of that day. When speaking with his accusers, he did not get trapped into the narrow focus on the adulterous behavior of the Samaritan woman or the dishonest practices of the tax collector Zacchaeus.

Jesus' perspective was rather at the deeper level of meaning and purpose for living: What caused these people to abuse human relationships? Once the deeper need was satisfied, there was no longer a reason for the sinful behavior; genuine repentance resulted. Jesus models for us here an acceptance of people where they are, with all of their flaws, without condoning their sinful behavior. He uses these behaviors as indicators of motivations that drive people.

Many people who come to pastors and counselors with sinful habits are primarily in need of security, love, and acceptance. They hope to find these qualities in a relationship with the Lord and his people. Pastors sell themselves short by overreacting to symptoms. They miss a unique opportunity to discover the deep needs that cause maladaptive behavior.

Pastors have more to offer than many nonpastoral counselors. Pastors can address the spiritual issues of meaning and purpose for life. Ministers usually have some history with the couple, perhaps understanding some of the issues that have brought on the idea of divorce. Also, the pastor has a ready-made community to support the couple in the difficult process of change. This is especially true if the church has cell groups in which people can pray and share intimately and develop strong, loving relationships with other believers. Such ongoing care groups would be the envy of many counselors in private practice who have to construct temporary support groups. Christian counselors could assist pastors in training cell group leaders in peer-counseling skills.

Adopting a counseling style does not mean pastors neglect the prophetic ministry. Rather, in ambidextrous fashion, the pastor shifts between prophetic and empathic styles, depending on the ministry situation. The preaching and teaching ministry can clarify the ideals of the Kingdom and motivate people to reach for those goals in their living. The counseling ministry, on the other hand, enables and guides. The minister shows people how to take ethical instruction from the lecture hall into the laboratory of life. This is where people will experiment (and, at times, make mistakes) as they try to apply some very difficult ideals to practical daily Christian living.

Christian ministers have their own understanding of justification and sanctification, knowing the tension between law and grace in the Scriptures. Unconfessed sin, which festers and becomes toxic over time, is still a bargain to the couple if confession will only lead to legalistic rejection and further pain.

The church sometimes has been viewed as a pure "holy club," only for those who have "arrived" spiritually. Its outreach is severely limited when it tries to embrace those who are experiencing failure of any kind. Christians facing problems are unlikely to share struggles about sin in their lives in this kind of setting for fear of alienation and rejection. And it's genuine fear that I've heard in people's voices, when they've said, "Pastor, if anyone in this church found out about . . . I would have to leave!" Preaching can focus on the goal of righteousness, but it has to be tempered with the message of God's grace.

Where grace is emphasized, there is an openness to share struggles and failures within the Christian community. There are no awkward silences when people cry out their heart's despair. "Tears are understood" and accepted. Time is given for wounded members to recover from their painful ordeals and begin to heal.

Like it or not, the pastor sets the tone and direction in the church. Through his lifestyle, preaching, teaching, and administration, the pastor indicates to the believers by his attitudes and remarks that it is safe to be genuine and honest with God's people.

Pastors and other counselors should ask themselves: "Am I creating an environment which encourages openness? Is this a place where people who have failed can reveal problems and receive forgiveness and acceptance?" A pastor may really have to work at creating this kind of loving environment, since many people have grown up believing that pastors are somehow "a different breed," sinless and perfect themselves. Wayne Oates shows the way this belief limits ministry:

In the mind of many people the minister is "not supposed to know" anything about the angers, the hostilities, the separations, and the irreconcilable differences that beset people. . . . Therefore, people tend to keep a minister carefully ignorant of their own hostile and inflamed relationships. . . . Too often the pastor is "the last to know." By the time the minister does become knowledgeable about the conflicts, they are "past the point of no return."[10]

I am convinced many marriages disintegrate because, at more teachable and treatable moments, couples don't feel safe to disclose their problems. Pastors recognize that "teachableness is the heart of marriage: unteachableness is the core of divorce."[11] No pastor or professional counselor wants to turn away a couple who is willing to learn, change and grow.

A Pastoral Dilemma

Pastors, since they are such visible leaders, face a real dilemma regarding divorce: No pastor wants to appear to be "pro divorce," at least not without serious qualifications! Even less desirable is earning the label of the "marrying Sam" for divorced people wanting to be remarried. There is a perception that to be "easy on divorce" puts one's spiritual credentials in question. As a result, many pastors avoid ministry to the divorced and divorcing altogether for the sake of their reputations (and perhaps for the sake of their church's and denomination's reputations, as well). So, then, may a pastor do "divorce counseling," or should he or she stick to "marriage counseling"? Consider Wayne Oates's comment: "Divorce counseling does not necessarily mean that we *advise* divorce. It does mean that we face the reality of divorce as one of the options that people increasingly choose in dealing with marital conflict."[12]

There's no escaping the growing number of divorced and remarried people who make up our communities. Have they committed an unpardonable sin that puts them outside the reach of the grace of God forever? Joyce Landorf Heatherley gives a searingly honest account of her own divorce in her book, *Unworld People:*

I believe having experienced the brokenness of divorce, that we have our absolutely golden opportunity to practice what we, with almost nauseating fervor, preach! As caring-dedicated-to-Christ-people, we should be constantly asking, "What Christ-like thought or gesture could I bring into someone's *unworld*, painful life to let them know they are loved and still of value to God and His people?[13]

Why do we treat divorced people differently from people struggling with any other category of social sin? It is probably that divorce, and particularly remarriage, present a unique category of falling short of the mark: God joined husband and wife in marriage, till death do them part. "What God has joined together, let man not separate" (Matt. 19:6 NIV). Do remarried individuals continue to sin as long as they live in a sexual relationship with someone else? Is a second or third marriage invalid in God's eyes?

If we believe this act of remarriage after divorce is categorically unpardonable, we very quickly write off thousands of people in the church as permanently outside of God's grace and forgiveness. What possible ministry can we have to couples married after divorce? Do we help people who have failed at marriage to be restored to full membership in the church? Or do we accord them a kind of second-class citizenship? Do we by our lack of love continue to make sin a bargain for those who sinned through divorce?

Sin is a bargain only as we allow it to be. If we had Jesus' eyes, we'd see the heavy load of guilt and hopelessness many couples carry. But many Christians have learned how to keep such ugly baggage politely hidden, especially around other believers. So, how can we make the pursuit of righteousness a better bargain? When people are liberated by God's love and grace, and accepted into a redemptive community of believers, it often becomes a bad deal to continue in sin! Why endure the tyranny and bondage of sin when one can be free through Christ Jesus and in fellowship with his people? The old gospel song, "At Calvary," says it well:

Years I spent in vanity and pride,
Caring not my Lord was crucified,
Knowing not it was for me He died on Calvary.

By God's Word at last my sin I learned;
Then I trembled at the law I'd spurned,
Till my guilty soul imploring turned to Calvary.

Now I've giv'n to Jesus ev'rything,
Now I gladly own Him as my King,
Now my raptured soul can only sing of Calvary.
Mercy there was great, and grace was free;
Pardon there was multiplied to me;
There my burdened soul found liberty, at Calvary.

POSSIBILITIES FOR CHANGE

Christian counselors can see beyond surface issues to genuine needs. Sometimes people know only sinful ways to satisfy needs for security, love, self-esteem, and self-fulfillment. Pastors can remind individuals that every legitimate need has a lawful means of fulfillment. The pastor as counselor encourages couples to find godly ways to have these needs met, by submitting themselves to the care and love of the Lord and his church. Then any pursuit of security, love, self-esteem, and self-fulfillment is under the control of God's Spirit, providing a balanced diet emotionally for those whose appetites have been out of control.

Often, counselors can demythologize sinful behavior by determining what drives people to take unethical and immoral shortcuts. Usually some legitimate goal or need has been blocked or jammed, and a person loses hope that this need can be met by conventional and lawful means.

A number of years ago, I did a counseling internship in a maximum security prison. Over a period of six months, I interviewed prisoners who had committed such crimes as tax evasion, burglary, auto theft, rape, extortion, and murder. Almost all of the prisoners had two things in common: First, they had an overwhelming desire to get something (money, revenge, acceptance, love) and an inability to get it as a law-abiding citizen. Second, they lost hope that their desires could ever be fulfilled lawfully. They decided to take an illegal shortcut to their goal.

They all took terrible risks, knowing they would probably get caught. They lacked the energy and perseverance to take the long way around the block; the shortcut was a better deal. After they had been caught and sent to prison, some admitted their impatience drove them to do the criminal acts. In their hopelessness, sin became a bargain.

When it comes to the issue of divorce, many people have what seem to them to be overwhelming needs. Spouses don't seem willing or able to satisfy these desires, and the marriage partner loses hope. Or when expectations are not met, husbands and wives search elsewhere.

A loving thing pastors and counselors can do is to help clients see that they are setting their partners up with godlike expectations that they can't fulfill. Spouses are human, after all! Though they bear the image of God, they also suffer from the limitations of a fallen world. Couples have placed their spouses where God rightly belongs. They have expected marriage partners to be what only God can be: Their ultimate source of security and love in an unloving and unpredictable world.

Often, this leads to a sense of isolation and hopelessness. Soon partners doubt God's character or capabilities in their marriage. If you believe God does not care or is not truly capable, then a choice to live as though he doesn't exist becomes reasonable, though painful.

Then pursuing immorality becomes a bargain! Chasing after the gods of money, sex, status, and power provides the necessary anesthesia to mask the pain of loneliness.

Psychologists, operating out of a humanistic framework, can trivialize or completely ignore a couple's spiritual and religious perceptions. They tend to concentrate on interpersonal relationships or communication skills development only, leaving religious issues to pastors and Christian counselors. This world view can be restrictive and can obscure significant clues to human behavior.

Pastors, on the other hand, see the spiritual dimension more clearly. But they often struggle with the complex process of untangling wounded human relationships. There is an intense desire on the part of pastors to help counselees deal with compound relational problems and correct sinful behavior. The difficulty is that these complex problems take time away from other ministries. There is an impatience to get on with the task of the church.

Somehow, through counseling, preaching, and teaching, we need to practice a holistic treatment plan, one which restores people relationally, both with God and with man. We have to show that growth and maturity in the Christian life is "a long obedience in the same direction."[14]

Behind our needs and desires stands an evil personality, Satan himself, influencing events and actions. That does not mean we are mere robots able to be manipulated at will. Rather, it openly acknowledges that the Evil One can take our natural desires and normal urges and lead us into arenas that God never intended for us. Old Testament Scripture is filled with evidence of such influence, from the first sin of Eve in the Garden of Eden (Gen. 3:1–13), to the story of Job (Job 1:6–2:10). The New Testament describes the same active evil influence upon the hearts of man, in the temptation of Christ (Matt. 4:1–11), in the teaching of Jesus on the Mount of Olives (Matt. 24–25), in the writings of Paul (Eph. 6:10–20), and in John's Revelation (Rev. 20:7–10).

Anyone who has been involved in Christian counseling recognizes this influence in the lives of their clients. This is not to label every action demonic. We only acknowledge Satan's oppressive power in the lives of some clients as a destructive force which cannot be explained in any other manner.

The well-known psychiatrist and author M. Scott Peck, in his book *People of the Lie: The Hope for Healing Human Evil,* tells of his dealings with this intrinsically evil influence in the life of one of his clients. He concluded that the wickedness evidenced could only be explained in supernatural terms.[15] It is impossible to look at the Holocaust of the 1940s or the Khmer Rouge slaughter of Cambodians in the 1970s without sensing a demonic component behind such extensive outbreaks of evil. Purely humanistic or psychological models provide feeble explanations for such mass madness.

In looking at statistics on the divorced and divorcing, one cannot help but see this evil influence upon our homes and our society. While we may not find a devil behind every bush (and, thereby, provide a scapegoat for human behavior), there does remain a power in our world which tempts men and women to destroy their relationships with one another and with the God above.

There is a better way of dealing with the pain and failure of the divorced and the divorcing. We can make it a bargain to seek forgiveness, restoration, and new life after such a painful experience. If we come to a better understanding of God's grace and love in the midst of our human failure, there will be life after divorce!

CHAPTER THREE

THE CRITICISMS OF DIVORCE

WHAT'S WRONG WITH IT?

Robert Schuller, pastor of the Crystal Cathedral in Garden Grove, California, repeatedly encourages viewers of his nationally televised program, "Hour of Power," not to view difficulties as problems. They are opportunities! He calls his people to view life positively with "possibility thinking," turning would-be disasters, with God's help, into spiritual victories.

If ever there was an opportunity for the church, it lies in the area of addressing the problem it has with divorce. There are few more controversial or divisive issues in twentieth century church life than the problems raised by divorce and the divorcing.

Responses to divorced and remarried individuals have a wide range, all the way from treating them as criminals who have committed capital crimes, to treating them as perpetrators of minor misdemeanors. Clergy and counselors often polarize on this issue. They experience significant role conflict in caring for hurting individuals while being responsible for the larger concerns of the Christian community.

Christians who take the Bible seriously as the sole guide for faith, life, and work are confronted with a difficult textual problem. How do we harmonize the rather explicit prohibitions regarding divorce in God's Word with its widespread practice in our society?

BIBLICAL STATEMENTS ON DIVORCE

The Bible addresses the issue of divorce in several significant passages in both the Old and New Testaments. Divorce was man's idea, designed by Moses to end marital acrimony and the evil consequences of sexual irresponsibility and abandonment.[1] Jesus reminded his disciples that divorce was the result of the hardness of men's hearts and was never intended to be God's perfect will: "Jesus replied, 'Moses permitted you to divorce your wives because your hearts were hard. But it was not this way from the beginning'" (Matt. 19:8).

In fact, the prophet Malachi addresses God's attitude toward capricious divorce: "Because the Lord hath been witness between thee and the wife of thy youth, against whom thou has dealt treacherously . . . For the Lord, the God of Israel, saith that he hateth putting away" (Mal. 2:14–16 KJV). Jesus further elaborates in Matthew 5:32 and Matthew 19:9 that anyone who puts his wife away, except for sexual unfaithfulness, commits adultery, and whoever marries a person divorced for other than adulterous reasons, commits adultery against that partner's spouse.[2]

The apostle Paul likewise makes a strong case against divorce. In Romans 7:1–4, Paul outlines a woman's responsibility to remain married to her husband as long as he lives; only at his death is she released from the marriage bond and permitted to remarry. In 1 Corinthians 7:10–15, Paul addresses Christian and non-Christian marriages. Where both parties are Christians, they are bound for life. If one partner departs, the other is to remain single with an eye to eventual reconciliation (vv. 10–11). Where only one mate is a Christian and his or her partner is not, the Christian is to dwell with the non-Christian spouse as long as the unbeliever desires. However, if the unbelieving person departs, and, in essence, abandons the Christian spouse, the Christian should let that husband or wife go. For the sake of peace they cease to be bound in that case (vv. 13–15).

The Bible esteems the marriage covenant. The only valid reasons for breaking the marriage covenant by divorce in God's eyes are those cases involving adultery (Matt. 5:32 and Matt. 19:9) and abandonment (1 Cor. 7:15). Outside of those very specific circumstances, covenant breaking is illegitimate and an act of rebellion and sin against God.

In summary, the difficulty we have with divorce is not that we do not understand these passages in Scripture, but, rather, that we have difficulty applying this unequivocal stance against the widespread practice of divorce.

We are reminded of what Abraham Lincoln is alleged to have said when asked about problems of interpreting Scripture: "It isn't what I do not understand that bothers me, but rather that which I do understand but don't do!" We, like Lincoln, have trouble with the application phase of the biblical teaching regarding divorce. We can understand why the disciples, after hearing Jesus' teaching on the subject, concluded it was better not to marry (Matt. 19:10).

INTERPRETATIONS ON DIVORCE

The problems of interpretation are more contextual than textual. Various attempts have been made to understand the hard statements against divorce in Scripture. For example, William Heth and Gordon Wenham support their conservative views with the argument that the majority of the early church fathers supported an antidivorce/remarriage position of the church.[3] They argue that tradition—a reinforcement of Christ's and the apostles' teaching—strongly supports their position. They contend that the sixteenth century Reformers and their followers (as a result of Erasmus's teaching on divorce) took a more liberal attitude,[4] which is popularized in the church today.

The early church view does not assume incoherence or inconsistency in the recorded teaching of Jesus in Matthew 19, contradictions between Jesus and the evangelists, between Paul and the evangelists, or between the teaching of the New Testament and the early Church. According to the early Church view, Jesus rejected the Jewish notions of divorce, and his teaching was followed by the gospel writers, St. Paul and the early Church fathers. . . . The teaching of the early Church fathers . . . cannot be reinterpreted to permit remarriage after divorce.[5]

Heath and Wenham, in their application of Scripture, declare that God provides grace to live according to a higher standard and to be an example of supernatural love in the midst of unrequited love and unfaithfulness.[6]

Geoffrey Bromiley, professor at Fuller Theological Seminary, agrees with this approach, saying:

What God requires must come before all else, the good as well as the bad. The followers of Jesus must be ready, should he will, to renounce even marriage for the sake of the gospel. They must be ready to obey God and not remarry after separation, even though they might plead, as often they do, that they have a right to happiness or to the fulfillment of natural desires. To talk of a right to happiness is to delude oneself. Happiness, when it is attained, is a gift from God and it cannot be attained, nor can human life be fulfilled, where there is conflict with God's stated will or a defiant refusal to see true happiness and fulfillment lie only in a primary commitment to God's kingdom and righteousness. For God's sake some people may have to forego marriage, some may have to put it in a new perspective, and some who have broken their marriage may have to refrain from remarriage. Marriage is a good thing, but it is not "the one thing needful" (Luke 10:42). Hence it may be—and in some instances it may have to be—surrendered.[7]

These writers, representing this conservative position, recognize that their interpretation of Scripture may be hard to accept, because its application is so painful for those seeking counsel. Yet, they hold the long view, rather than a more temporal view: Self-fulfillment and quality of life are humanistic ideas which can divert a person from doing God's will and experiencing eternal life. Their rationale is "God gives grace and power to do God's will, so do it!" The faithful ought to remain faithful and not divorce or remarry. Thus pastoral concern takes a preventive orientation rather than a rehabilitative approach to divorce.

The Reformers and many modern theologians have taken a more liberal approach toward the divorced. They have accepted a less-than-ideal world. They see people corrupted by sin, living at various levels of spiritual development and maturity. This has resulted in intervention and rehabilitation programs for the divorced.

The Reformation leader Martin Luther addressed in detail the exception clauses for divorce on the grounds of adultery and desertion. He believed Scripture allows for remarriage in both cases, based on an argument that adultery and abandonment imply death, both toward God and the marital partner:

> Luther states emphatically that Christ allowed divorce only in the case of adultery and desertion. The Christian who is deserted by an unbelieving partner may marry again as long as the future husband is a Christian. From this he concludes that the innocent party in any divorce case be allowed to marry again, such as a wife whose husband deserts her or returns after ten years. . . .
>
> His starting point is that only death can dissolve the marriage tie and leave the partner free to marry again. The act of adultery, however, makes the offender as dead in his relationship both to God and to his partner. . . .
>
> If a Christian husband is such a rascal that he leaves his believing wife and children, then he should be considered no better than a gentile or an unbeliever and deserves the punishment due to the adulterer. Since Paul, in Luther's view, permits the believing partner to marry again, Luther sees no reason why this should not be true in this case also.[8]

The biblical grounds for legitimate divorce (adultery and abandonment) remained the same with the Reformers and later theologians, but a strong case was made to establish innocence, and, concurrently, the right to remarry while one's spouse is still alive.

Once their innocence is established, individuals have the freedom to remarry, as Guy Duty states in his book *Divorce and Remarriage*:

> God believed there were innocent parties in Old Testament times. We saw in Numbers 5:12–31 that when God cursed the guilty wife whose husband suspected her of adultery, the husband was held "guiltless." Moses believed there were innocent parties, because he killed the guilty and set the innocent free. . . . Jesus must have believed there were innocent parties or He would not have given us the fornication exception.[9]

Evidently, in God's eyes, the original marriage was dissolved, allowing the innocent party to remarry.

Most counselors cringe at the term "innocent party," because they have seen so many couples where both partners have contributed to the death of the marriage. Yet, for ethicists and judicial authorities, innocence (even relative innocence) is a genuine category.

THEOLOGICAL PROBLEMS WITH DIVORCE

There are some theological problems with divorce. These relate to Christian doctrines of sin and grace and the marriage covenant.

The problem with so many theological theories on divorce is that they are hard to apply in the counselor's office. Most writing on divorce has addressed only a very narrow spectrum of this population, namely those who have been abandoned or those whose spouses have committed adultery. Yet, what about the thousands of others who have divorced on other than biblical grounds?

A large percentage of the divorcing and the divorced have not been abandoned nor have their spouses committed adultery against them. In short, from a biblical perspective, they have failed to follow God's plan for marriage and have sinned against him and their marriage partner. They have broken communication lines and commitment bonds.

What does the church have to say to such persons, who feel like such failures before God? (Their logic is simple: "Divorce is failure. I am divorced. Therefore, I am a failure."[10]) What is the nature of their sin? Is it possible for them to be forgiven and be restored to fellowship with God and his people?

These are the kinds of people who pastors see every day in their ministries. They include all of the following: 1) conflicted couples who have decided the only escape from their pain and struggle is divorce; 2) the abandoned or victimized who want a new start; 3) the divorced who desire to marry again, and 4) blended families suffering confusion and conflict in their relationship.

Theologians struggle with judicial issues of guilt or innocence, hoping to maintain the purity of the church and prevent divorce. Pastors struggle with the consequences of immorality, hoping to restore couples to spiritual and psychological wholeness. It is not enough to portray the ideal; we must come to grips with the real! For that, we have to examine our theology of sin and grace as it applies to divorce.

Pastors know of the widespread effects of the Fall upon human relationships. Sin has taken its toll on marriages, as well as on all other aspects of life. Once sin entered the world, men and women embraced and endorsed rebellion against God's will and proceeded to do their own thing.[11] The selfishness in the heart of mankind insists upon its own way. This self-centeredness is the primary component of every kind of sin. It is found in every immoral and wicked action of mankind.

In fact, we have great difficulty appreciating the depth to which sin is found, even in the hearts of the redeemed. Much of our disillusionment over marital failure in the church is rooted in our shallow grasp of how deeply evil has taken root and remained alive in the lives of people. In one sense, we should be surprised that Kingdom ethics survive at all. It requires God's grace to make the choice to live selflessly in a selfish world.

Many psychologists view sinful behavior in more humanistic terms, distinguishing self-esteem from excessive self-love or narcissism. "Erich Fromm, Alfred Adler, Abraham Maslow and Carl Rogers all emphasized that an individual with healthy self-esteem is rarely selfish."[12]

Both Christian theology and psychology see selfism as the source for a lot of human conflict. Both see the need for spiritual and psychological maturity to deal with sinfully destructive issues in life. Both acknowledge that great evil can come from selfism.

They differ, however, in that theologians see this primarily in moral terms: Selfishness is willful rebellion against God. Psychologists see this in behavioral terms: Selfishness is immaturity and offensiveness toward one's fellow human beings. Rather than look at the sin issue in "either-or" terms (sin as willful rebellion or simple immaturity), most pastors are comfortable combining the two theories. That is, sin involves acts of disobedience which may stem from psychological and spiritual immaturity.

Christian pastors and other Christian counselors continue to be concerned with encouraging kingdom ethics. However, the problem is that stressing ethics without acknowledging human need contributes to religious legalism and schizophrenic behavior. Stressing human need without morality leads to lawlessness and selfishness.

Perhaps the church has lost the balance in the Reformation teaching on law and grace. Luther taught that the law is a schoolmaster who brings us to Christ. It is law which confronts us with our dire need for God's grace. The law shows the goal to be reached, while grace enables us to move toward that goal.

Counselors cannot expect instant perfection! God's grace is essential in the process of sanctification. But many people assimilate truth mostly through the trial-and-error method, and that tends to be a slow process. It can be frustrating to those counselors who see a need for mature Christian workers.

Psychologists appreciate the process of growth and enjoy watching the interaction of people as they move toward greater maturity. But they tend to be uncertain about the goal of "spiritual maturity."

The parable of the cancer researchers will illustrate this difference. One group of researchers (the theologians) come to the laboratory with a well-defined goal—to discover the cause of cancer and defeat it. What they lack is the patience to stick with the process of mixing various solutions in their test tubes, and, through trial and error, to narrow the field of inquiry. Their tendency is to become impatient if they do not quickly discover the cause of cancer. They do not fully appreciate the fact that failure may be educational.

The other group of researchers (the counselors) come to the lab highly motivated to work there. They love the camaraderie of the workplace and enjoy the research process with its various slides to be examined under microscopes. Yet, in spite of their love for the process of inquiry, they are never quite sure of their goals. There is great tolerance for experimentation, but not so much urgency to complete the research task. In short, one group is goal-oriented, while the other is process-oriented.

Each group of researchers can learn from the other: 1) to have a clearly developed goal, with 2) measurable milestones, while 3) being tolerant of the process, and 4) being appreciative of the educational role of the trial-and-error method. The ultimate goal for both is to help couples become more Christlike through counseling.

THE REAL SIN OF DIVORCE

Another theological issue associated with divorce is the sin of covenant breaking, which is really how divorce can be defined. When two people marry, they make a covenant of faithfulness to each other, with God as a witness of that vow. If that covenant is violated by one or both partners, the relationship is put in jeopardy.

Dwight Small broadens the scope of inquiry beyond just adultery and abandonment as the sole ways of breaking the marriage covenant:

> Whenever a spouse is aware of being no longer committed to covenant goals or obligations, to marital unity as total partnership, or to a loving mutuality, then the covenant is beginning to come apart. . . . There is a sense in which marriage

can die. Covenant unity can be broken because one or both spouses walk away from its obligations or turn off mentally or emotionally in what becomes tantamount to a repudiation of the covenant. All too often an internal repudiation precedes the more visible external conflict. . . . It comes down to the choices we make, or continue to make. We choose to remain faithful to the covenant—or not to. . . . Faithless actions and attitudes often precede by some length of time that moment when it all spills over into a new attraction, say, or an extramarital affair. Sexual infidelity then is the symptom, not the cause. Divorce then merely gives decent burial to the marriage that died—or was murdered![13]

Many counselors are more comfortable with this broader approach to the causes of divorce; they view acts of abandonment or adultery as overt results of progressive sinning against the marriage covenant.

"Not all marriages among professing Christians are Christian marriages. . . . They do not all meet the standard God sets; they are not all covenants of unity and fidelity representative of Christ and His church. They do not all follow the role structure laid down in Scripture. Nor do they all look to God for His empowering for their success. In fact, many are merely Christian in name only."[14] Consequently, covenant breaking that leads to divorce is more broadly defined than overt acts of adultery or abandonment. The process of divorce really begins much sooner, either because there is no distinctly Christian foundation to the marriage or because of a variety of willful acts of recklessness and negligence against the marriage covenant.

In my experience, the words "reckless" and "negligent" sound overly harsh when describing many couples' careless behavior: the little, seemingly inconsequential, choices that cumulatively take them off the course of marital success. James Dobson says,

The same circumstances that destroy non-Christian marriages can also be deadly in the homes of believers. I'm not referring to alcoholism or infidelity or compulsive gambling. The most common marriage killer is much more subtle and insidious.[15]

In his book, *Straight Talk to Men and Their Wives,* Dobson goes on to describe this "killer" as an overcommitted, workaholic husband, and a depressed, lonely wife, who become increasingly disillusioned with each other and their roles as husband/ wife, provider/nurturer, and dad/mom. Finally, the day comes when the futility and hopelessness of it all really hit them, and they just throw it all away.

Jason Towner described the gradual breakdown of his marriage this way: "We did not fight or loudly disagree, but in our spirits we did not meet. There was no communication, no communion."[16] Such unintentional carelessness can be viewed as the real sin which breaks the covenant.

THE ISSUE OF REMARRIAGE

Writers are divided when it comes to the issues of divorce and remarriage. Heth and Wenham and J. Carl Laney take the conservative position that only death dissolves a marriage covenant; therefore, remarriage is out of the question, for it involves adultery against the former partner. Guy Duty claims exceptions are allowed for remarriage for the innocent party of a marriage which ended in divorce by reason of adultery or abandonment. Jay Adams and Dwight Small believe remarriage is possible once the marriage covenant is broken by divorce and offenders seek forgiveness for their action (whether the divorce was on biblical grounds or not). Both Adams and Small argue that God's grace is greater than the sin of divorce. (Further examination of the writings of all these authors is recommended for a much more comprehensive discussion of this issue of divorce and remarriage.)

If one or both parties has already remarried, the relationship is irreconcilably severed and impossible to restore. In cases such as this, forgiveness from the former spouse should be pursued and efforts must be made to build a Christian marriage in the new relationship. The rationale for this is not an argument to insure *happiness* as much as it is to encourage couples to pursue *holiness.*

In no way should divorce be considered an "unpardonable sin," since there really is no scriptural reference for such a position. In fact, Paul writes in 1 Corinthians 6:9–11, "Do you not know that the wicked will not inherit the Kingdom of God? Do not be deceived: Neither the sexually immoral, nor idolaters, nor adulterers, . . . will inherit the Kingdom of God. And that is what some of you *were*. But you were washed, you were sanctified, you were justified in the Name of the Lord Jesus Christ and by the Spirit of our God." Jay Adams, in particular, underlines this when he states:

> Let us make clear, then, that those who wrongly (sinfully) obtain a divorce must not be excused for what they have done; it is sin. But precisely because it is sin, it is forgivable. The sin of divorcing one's mate on unbiblical grounds is bad, not only because of the misery it occasions, but because it is an offense against a holy God. But it is not so indelibly imprinted in the life of the sinner that it cannot be washed away by Christ's blood. . . . Since divorce is not the unpardonable sin, it can be forgiven. That, of course, does not heal all the heartbreaks of children and in-laws, not to speak of the parties involved in the divorce. . . . Divorce, even when proper, always is occasioned by someone's sin. At its best, then, divorce always brings misery and hurt. That is why God hates it. . . . We must not call unclean those whom God has cleansed. . . . The only sin that never can be forgiven is the sin of attributing the work of the Holy Spirit to an unclean spirit.[17]

A CHALLENGE FOR THE CHURCH

Though divorce is not the unpardonable sin, pastors will attempt to prevent it in every way possible. Preventive care programs involve preaching and teaching on the specifics of Christian marriage. This includes practical experiences such as Marriage Encounter, Marriage Enrichment, and various types of premarital counseling. Most of these stress dialogue between spouses and expression of loving feelings. Any program which encourages couples to clarify goals and sharpen their communication skills has long-range value. Intervention programs, through cell groups and support groups, should be ongoing and well-publicized. Pastors should make it clear that these programs are not so much for disintegrating marriages as they are for healthy relationships. They are designed to make good marriages better.

In all of our ministries, it is important to proclaim two truths as clearly as we can: 1) God's plan is for us to live holy lives, seeking to please him in all our attitudes and actions, and supporting each other in this pursuit, and 2) God's grace is available for forgiveness and empowerment to live as we ought, even in the pain of failure. When we teach both of these truths, we lead our churches in a balanced approach toward the divorced and the divorcing.

This is not to "go soft" on divorce by any means. But where people fail, we work to restore them to fellowship with God and his people. When divorced people apply for membership in the church, circumstances should be reviewed: Can this partner's innocence be determined? In the case of an unbiblical divorce, is there genuine repentance? Have church members who have been involved in a wrongful divorce now submitted to church discipline and accountability? By all of these means, divorced individuals reestablish credibility for fellowship and service.

If repentance is thought to be genuine and the fruit of the Holy Spirit is evident in a person's life, fellowship should never be denied. All of us belong to a community of sinners saved by grace. It is appropriate, however, that efforts be made to confront issues which caused the marriage to fail. Perhaps we can help to prevent further relational failures for this same person or others in similar circumstances.

Such a stance does not contradict the church's call to its people to live holy lives for the Lord, separated from the world. It merely acknowledges that we live in a fallen world where sinful behavior dies hard. When people do not fully understand nor appropriate God's grace to live the Christian life, they fall into sin. We merely proclaim God's provision to restore such a one to fellowship with himself and his church.

Divorce and remarriage are a challenge for the church. They provide a real opportunity for ministry to a large segment of

society comprised of those who often perceive themselves outside of the grace of God. Couples considering divorce may avoid
the church because they believe a pastor will only attempt to
have them reconcile. Divorced people who grew up in the
church assume that they will be rejected. They feel isolated
from the Body of believers and sometimes grieve more than
people who have suffered the death of a loved one.

> The rituals of a divorce situation differ from those associ-
> ated with death in being so isolated; often they are totally
> devoid of any formal community expression. Divorce is that
> form of grief for which there are no flowers sent, no church
> ceremonies offered to help persons come to grips with the
> reality and finality of the separation. The community tends
> to be brought together by death, but divided—scattered—
> by divorce.[18]

I believe the Lord would want us to welcome these "prodigals"
back to his house and to fellowship with his people.

Our world needs to see the standards of righteousness modeled by a godly remnant. But it also needs to see God's people
compassionately reaching out to those who have fallen away
from that ideal. Our message must be a gracious one, humbly
sensitive to God's love and forgiveness toward all. Divorce, like
every sin, is never without painful consequences. However, we
do not let people remain spiritually alienated in order to punish
them or let them serve as an object lesson to the rest of the
flock!

As Dwight Small says:

> The essential point is that grace does not invite presumptu-
> ousness. Grace is the great incentive to live for the smile of
> the One who is gracious to us. Those who fear that grace
> will lead to presumptuousness fail to reckon with the na-
> ture and power of grace or with the convicting ministry of
> the Holy Spirit. . . . Grace plants the desire for holiness
> in our hearts![19]

CHAPTER FOUR

SOME PICTURES OF DIVORCE

WHO ARE THESE PEOPLE?

People get divorced! If you pasted on the wall a collage of snap-shots of all the people you know who got divorced, what would it look like? Would the faces have a particular "hardened" look like those found on "Wanted" posters at the post office? Proba-bly not! They are just people: some attractive, others not so good-looking; some intelligent, others not so smart; some suc-cessful, others not so well off.

All have in common the painful look of loss. We are not just discussing the theology or ethics of divorce as some vague ab-straction. We are talking about *real* people—people who laugh and cry, who have parents who love them, or children of their own.

Who are they? They are our neighbors, our co-workers, our friends, and relatives. They are not just found among the disadvantaged but also among the affluent. They are not only in the world, but also in the church! As Dobson writes, "Perhaps you know that the divorce rate in America is now higher than in any other civilized nation in the world. . . . That is tragic. Even more distressing to me is knowledge that the divorce rate for Christians is only slightly lower than for the population at large."[1] According to Mary LaGrand Bouma, not so long ago, a divorced politician couldn't get elected, and pastors couldn't minister if they'd been divorced. She says, "The last defense against this social disorder was the clergy,"[2] but now most of us can name one or two or three ministers we know who are divorced.

If we are going to talk about divorce, we are going to be talking about people—people who need love, not rejection; people who need healing, not more hurt; people who need a Savior.

I want to look at five composite sketches, drawn from hundreds of couples which typify categories of the divorced and the divorcing. Obviously, names were chosen to insure anonymity.

JOHN AND CAROL: SURPRISED BY DIVORCE

John and Carol are typical of the couple surprised by divorce. Carol's Bible-study leader encourages her to see a Christian counselor since she is so emotionally distraught and mentally confused. She just had a blowup with John, her husband of seventeen years. Carol discovered that John was having numerous affairs during out-of-town business trips.

She thinks, *I could try to understand one brief sexual encounter. But John has betrayed me again and again. I just can't forgive him for what he has done.* She orders John out of the house and tells him she wants a divorce.

Carol appears in the counselor's office and tearfully gushes out her sense of pain, anger, and betrayal. "How could he do this to me? To us?" Divorce is the only way out of a marriage broken beyond repair, according to Carol. She sees most of the life she constructed as a supportive wife and mother now lying in ruin. And it's not just anger she is feeling; she experiences intense grief over what could have been, but now will never be.

Fear emerges as she faces the possibility of major financial and social changes in her life and in the lives of her two teenage children. They've lived in a comfortable home in the best part of town. Her sense of security is gone. Will she ever be able to trust anyone again? Bitterness seeps down to the depths of her heart. Once poised and attractive, Carol now looks disheveled and unkempt.

John comes begrudgingly to counseling, out of a sense of obligation, he says. "I guess I owe this much to Carol." He is depressed and feeling guilty; yet, he is somewhat ambivalent about his future. He had hoped, of course, that Carol would not discover his infidelity, but he is not very sorry the affairs happened. The guilt is largely focused on the pain he has caused Carol, who has remained so supportive and faithful to him. "I didn't mean to hurt her this much," he says.

He, too, is surprised at the untimely nature of a possible divorce. The financial and emotional investment now looks mountainous to him. Yet, he, more than Carol, has been aware of the barrenness in their relationship. "I don't know how she could be happy with so little going for us." He says he sought diversionary affairs as a way of spicing up his life. He didn't plan to sabotage the respectable life he and Carol have built for themselves. He knows divorce will force some major changes in his rather well-ordered life. "When I think about my future, I'm scared and excited at the same time," he admits. He tries very hard to keep his emotions under control.

This couple is held in a destructive deadlock. Carol says, "I cannot forgive John for his betrayal." She sees divorce as the only acceptable way to retain some sense of pride and integrity. Mostly she feels anger and self-pity. John doesn't really want to repent and return to the marriage. "What would change? My life with Carol is dull." The primary motivator driving him is his fear that he is getting older and has to "go for the gusto" before it is gone forever.

The real threat of divorce may be a surprise for both John and Carol. Though Carol says she wasn't aware of the breakdown of her marriage, there must have been numerous indications that theirs was not a healthy relationship. Somewhere along the way, the fire of romance went out, and with it any shared goals and dreams for them to pursue. They somehow slipped into a comfortable but boring existence. Considering the minimal effort they were expending on their marriage, it's really no wonder it is feeble and dying. And now, problems that could have been dealt with much less expensively months or years earlier may have put the marriage beyond repair.

John's and Carol's crisis represents to the Christian counselor a marriage seriously threatened by neglect that led to adultery. Whether it can be repaired will depend upon how willing each one is to renegotiate the marriage compact and work at a process of renewal.

Of the several categories of marital conflict we will examine, surprisingly, this one has the greatest potential for restoration. The counselor knows—and tries to convince this couple—that no relationship survives without some effort. The primary risk is that one or both partners will just not believe the marriage is worth the struggle it will take to restore it.

In the case of John and Carol, I'll want to observe whether they both recognize the affairs as symptomatic of a deeper problem. For Carol, there will have to come a sense of ownership of her part in allowing the marriage to get stale and boring without serious protest. Can she accept the fact that John's behavior was related to a growing fear over impending age, impotence, and death? Can she even begin to forgive John and try to allow a new beginning?

John, on the other hand, has to admit his contribution to the conflict. His sexual indiscretions were hurtful to Carol; but even more harmful to their marriage was the dishonesty which became a part of his life. He has to recognize the work of trust-building which will be largely his responsibility if they are to repair their marriage. He also needs to grapple with the spiritual issue of his infidelity. He, like Carol, will have to learn the art of seeking, receiving, and offering forgiveness—of each other and from the Lord.

All of these tasks are large ones, but not impossible. Carol can refuse to forgive John. She can even be justified in divorcing

John according to biblical principles, since he has committed adultery.

John needs to offer more than half-hearted repentance. If he doesn't accept his own mortality, he will either stay miserably with Carol or go back to younger women as a way to rejuvenate himself and deny his aging.

John's business traveling may have contributed to the problems; but according to him, that wasn't the issue. The problem was boredom. Many airline pilots, military personnel, and businessmen travel from home frequently and have good marriages. As Jason Towner, author of *Jason Loves Jane, But They Got a Divorce,* states: "The separation does not always cause marital problems; it merely means you are not home to deal with the problem."[3] In fact, some marriages may be prolonged by frequent absences. The partners are separated so much of the time, they can almost live like singles while maintaining the respectability of staying married.

The separations made it easier for John not to deal with the barrenness of his relationship with Carol. This made him vulnerable to having an affair. As Dr. Dobson writes, "A man and a woman commit adultery when they are emotionally ready for it."[4] John is still so thrilled with the excitement of his new sense of freedom that he probably doesn't realize that life may not be necessarily better, just different.

In summary, some of the significant issues in John's and Carol's situation are the following: Efforts need to be made in the assessment phase of counseling to determine if John is motivated to work on the marriage. If he really has lost interest in a relationship with Carol, other than her being the mother of his children, continued counseling is a waste of time. The affairs would probably continue—an unacceptable situation to Carol.

However, if John were willing to work on the marriage, to try to regain what has been lost, things might turn around. This couple must rediscover why they got married and what has been positive in their relationship.

John and Carol need to come to grips with life-cycle issues which cause them to respond to aging in negative ways. At root is an existential spiritual crisis: What is the meaning and purpose of my life? Will my life be over before I discover why I'm here? Rather than searching for the fountain of youth, both individuals need to appreciate the season of life they are in and value each other.

Carol will have to struggle anew with forgiveness, both as a single act now and as a process over the next few years. She will have to learn to trust again, while John learns to be trustworthy and shows that he can be trusted. If that happens, there is a good chance this marriage will resurrect.

RON AND ALLISON: CRISIS-FILLED MARRIAGE

Unlike John and Carol, Ron and Allison represent couples to whom divorce comes as no surprise. They married young (Ron was eighteen, Allison seventeen), and they had their first—and only—child within six months of the wedding. Both grew up in families filled with conflict, alcohol abuse, and physical/mental abuse. Both ran away from home into each other's arms after their parents had divorced and remarried spouses who had children of their own. Neither one completed high school and they have held low-paying, insecure employment, living from payday to payday. Neither Ron nor Allison has had healthy role models. They have few friends and no connection with the church except in sending their son Jeffrey to a church-sponsored day-care center and occasionally to Sunday school.

Ron and Allison are typical of a couple who present themselves to a counselor at a crisis point. Following an incident of abuse, Allison appears on the pastor's doorstep late one night with her son Jeffrey trailing behind her. It is important to note that the pastor often is a first-line intervention professional to assist abused spouses (along with healthcare specialists in public clinics and shelters). As such, the pastor's first priority is the safety of the mother and child. He or she eventually will become a resource person for the family as they try to make sense out of their lives.

After finding them a place in a spouse-abuse shelter, the pastor follows up on the situation a week later, when Allison is back home.

Allison tells the pastor, when he visits her small and dreary apartment, that the incident was not that unusual. They have endured years of cumulative arguments over money, relatives, lack of vocational opportunities, and the excessive use of alcohol and drugs. It quickly becomes evident that family violence is an habitual feature of this home. Tragically, both parents have repeatedly taken out their frustrations on their son as well as on each other. "But it always starts with Ron's drinking," Allison says. It does appear that the intensity of the violence is often in proportion to Ron's alcohol abuse.

To put it simply, this marriage has become as dangerous as it is confusing for all members. Allison says, "I can't believe I've gotten myself—and Jeffrey—into such a horrible mess." For the first time, she starts talking to someone (the pastor) about divorce, though she says she has thought about it at least a hundred times before. She is scared, not just for herself, but for Jeffrey as well. "Ron will kill me if I try to leave. He believes he 'owns' me and if he can't have me, no one will have me," she says, barely keeping her hysteria in check.

In my opinion, Ron's and Allison's case represents the most difficult marital situation with which to work. These are clients who will demand considerable resources both in time and effort. Both partners have had conflict-filled and abusive childhoods, lacking good role models for parenting or couple bonding. Marriage to each other was largely an attempt to escape their past, seeking emotional support from a partner. But that partner was also crippled by the circumstances of life. There was also the birth of a child immediately after marriage, with neither teenager prepared emotionally or financially for parenting responsibilities. Finally, add to this equation the deeply habituated patterns of alcohol and spouse/child abuse, and the counselor is confronted with a real disaster in process.

The counselor will wonder if there is any hope for such a couple to recover. Or does it seem clear that the primary help we can give will be to assist the couple in separating? That decision will depend on the inner strength of the couple and the availability of resources to assist them over an extended period of time. There are no quick fixes for such people. Genuine help will require a massive overhaul of their marriage. A supporting cast of psycho-socio-religious professionals must assist this couple in becoming mature individuals. Long-term treatment and support are going to be needed to break destructive habits and reinforce positive ways of conflict resolution.

When pastors do not feel fully adequate to meet this kind of challenge, they need to refer these couples to professional counselors skilled in behavior modification and chemical-dependency/spouse-abuse treatment. The pastoral relationship then becomes one of facilitating a team ministry for the couple and monitoring their progress. It is not wise for the pastor alone to try to minister to such a couple. From a practical standpoint, the time commitments will cause other aspects of the ministry to suffer. This is an ideal situation for pastors and Christian counselors to work together as a team.

The primary effort of getting Allison into a spouse-abuse shelter and Jeffrey under the care of child-protective services is important. Sometimes Christian counselors want to avoid bringing in state or county authorities and quietly shelter such victims on their own. In my estimation, that is a therapeutic mistake—as well as a legal error in many states. Pastors and other counselors may think they are being kind by not making this situation a public issue; but that is exactly why the problem has persisted so long—it has been kept private. By bringing the protective services into the picture, treatment resources become available and the threat of legal prosecution can be used to motivate Ron and Allison to enter treatment for their abusive behavior. Concurrently, the chemical-dependency problem is addressed with the necessary medical assistance assured. Counseling will be futile until the alcohol abuse is under control. Even the placement of Jeffrey in foster care until his parents can demonstrate to the court that they can care for him properly will be a great inducement to complete these treatment programs. Without such leverage, few couples would be motivated to work on their problems.

Ron and Allison represent couples that seemingly have overwhelmingly complex problems involving many aspects of their lives. A number of interrelated crises can stem from chemical dependency and spouse abuse.

For these reasons, Ron and Allison are less likely to succeed in counseling. Their own personal histories are against them: their abusive childhoods and their present abusive behavior, their lack of economic power and social skills, their lack of childrearing skills, and Ron's alcoholism. Short of intense behavior therapy that stops the alcoholism and spouse/child abuse, they will not get far. Only if they respond favorably to suggestions regarding anger control, communication skills, vocational-educational training, and the problems associated with chemical dependency is there hope for them.

For Ron and Allison, treatment is a process of education and reinforcement. They need to develop adult skills and responsibility in order to cope with life and enjoy each other. Therapy for them will be long-term, lasting as long as it takes them to build their own self-monitoring system.

If the pastor-counselor team can deal with the couple's deeply habituated problems, Ron's and Allison's marriage may be salvaged. Miracles do sometimes occur—and that's just about what it will take to rebuild this marriage.

LARRY AND JENNIFER: THE BLENDED-FAMILY MARRIAGE

Larry and Jennifer typify the third type of couple who seek counseling, those who come because they are exhausted from working on their marriages. This is the second marriage for both of them. Larry brought to the marriage two daughters, ages ten and thirteen; he married eight months after the accidental death of his first wife, Karen. Jennifer has a seven-year-old daughter and a nine-year-old son from her first marriage. She divorced an alcoholic and abusive husband three years ago.

Though both Larry and Jennifer present themselves as mature enough to handle a blended family, they express confusion and frustration at making their marriage work. They feel like it's just never going to get better. They suggest it's time to admit this marriage was a mistake and end the relationship as soon as possible.

Each tells the same story: "We've really tried to make it work. We really love each other, but our kids just haven't been able to accept us being together. We thought it would get better with time, but it seems like it's getting worse!"

In this case, the children have not blended well into the new family structure. They have used temper tantrums, disrespect, academic failure, and several episodes of running away to express their displeasure at the relationship. Larry's daughters, according to Jennifer, "Hate me! They won't let me be their mom!" Larry, knowing Jennifer is concerned about the problem, reports that he scolds his daughters for their rude behavior. Yet, with several runaway episodes, Larry is concerned over alienating and losing his daughters.

The big scare for Jennifer is that Larry's fears are affecting their relationship and she doesn't want to lose Larry and be divorced a second time. There is a tone of desperation in her voice when she says: "I *can't* fail at marriage again!" Jennifer's children, in contrast, have responded positively to Larry and to the violence-free environment. Problems involving them usually arise only after Nick, Jennifer's ex-husband, takes them for two weekends a month. When they return, they are difficult to manage. They constantly resent their mother's discipline, telling her, "Daddy is always so nice to us." Also, Nick repeatedly runs down Larry to the children. His efforts of playing "Santa Claus," giving gifts and good times to the children, makes Jennifer and Larry look bad when handling day-to-day discipline and chores. Jennifer's son has had a hard time getting close to Larry, although her daughter adores him. Meanwhile, Jennifer's children are ignored as much as possible by Larry's daughters. Jennifer complains, "They don't help me with my kids—they act like they don't even exist!"

Larry's in-laws from his first marriage (Karen's parents) are upset over his "hasty marriage" only eight months after the death of their daughter. They have made their dissatisfaction with Jennifer and her family well known. They also are irritated that they do not see more of their grandchildren. The grandparents have communicated to Larry's girls that they would love to have them come and live with them. The girls, in turn, use this as a threat whenever there is a blowup at home.

Larry's and Jennifer's home is very confusing, filled with a lot of fear, anger and a none-too-subtle struggle for power. Much of what a counselor hears from Larry and Jennifer is a large volume of information which needs to be organized. Through the use of family diagrams and a good psycho-social history, a lot of the confusing data can be organized into helpful patterns and trends. Often by seeing the forces which pull at them and influence them, the couple can tackle these issues.

One of the biggest problems in a stepfamily relationship like Larry's and Jennifer's is a struggle for power and control of the family system. The old divide-and-conquer method is used by those who desire to sabotage the relationship for their own self-serving ends.

My experience has been that couples like Larry and Jennifer have never clearly identified the tangle of relationships or the number of stresses they encounter. If the counselor can enable couples to face these external forces together, that joint effort can have a cohesive effect upon their marriage. A sense of hope can then be generated that can give the couple energy to enter into the work of family counseling.

The focus of care for Larry's and Jennifer's family should be not just on the couple, but on the entire immediate family. Since family therapy can be "busy" dynamically, it is helpful to have two counselors co-facilitating the sessions (some counselors suggest a male/female therapy team).

The counselor's task will be to understand this unique family system, comprehending family relationships, and utilizing a genogram (see page 136) of the family tree. It involves focusing on communication patterns which give clues about how family members feel about each other and who is valued by whom. Counseling gives Jennifer the opportunity to share her sense of isolation and Larry the chance to verbalize, in the girls' presence, his fear of losing his daughters. The objective is for the daughters to recognize their anger over the blending of these two families. During the sessions, one counselor has primary responsibility to monitor the counseling process (how the family is communicating verbally and non-verbally) while the other is primarily focusing on the content of what is expressed.

If the sessions lead to greater awareness of the problems and a recognition of a personal investment by all family members in the family enterprise, then recovery can be achieved in a relatively short time. Future sessions primarily will involve monitoring family progress in dealing with specific issues which lead to dysfunction.

The daughters' negative behavior may not change. If they are willing, they could benefit from a support group made up of other children from blended families. In some cases, couples like Jennifer and Larry may have to take some training and receive support from a "Toughlove"-type group. This will not change the children's behavior either, but it will provide coping skills for parents battered by abusive and angry children.

Family therapy is not for the unskilled. Pastors need to be aware of this very useful holistic approach to family conflict and have ready access to a counselor skilled in family systems. Any counselor wants to keep in mind that Larry's and Jennifer's problems are externally induced, systemic problems. To treat them as primarily psychological or spiritual is to miss the central issues.

For Larry and Jennifer, counseling will involve enabling them to sort out the confusing family pattern which confronts them, and teaching them to stand together against efforts to sabotage the relationship. Family therapy is indicated here; each family member will be confronted with his or her positive and negative contributions to the family system. The counselor doesn't want anyone left outside the counseling circle who has an investment to keep the system "sick." In counseling sessions, family members may role play particularly destructive or aggravating behavior. This reveals family secrets which everyone can then examine.

The success of counseling for Larry and Jennifer will be proportionate to the number of family members who genuinely participate in the process and who agree on some reasonable goals and objectives. The safety for family members to share their true feelings openly without being crushed by the rest of the family is a sign of health and progress.

Roger and Sally: The Claustrophobic Marriage

Roger and Sally suffer from emotional claustrophobia. Their pastor becomes aware of their problems when a mid-Saturday morning phone call interrupts a meeting. Roger, a Christian, announces that Sally has left him and may he please come over and talk. Upon arriving at the pastor's study, Roger begins to share his pain.

He says that he thought he had a good marriage for the past eight years. He and his wife Sally have two healthy children, ages six and four. Roger has been the breadwinner while Sally has stayed home and cared for the children. They live modestly, but lately they have experienced more problems than usual paying their bills. Sally decided to go back to work as a legal secretary, supposedly to help during the financial crunch. But Roger says, "She just used that as an excuse. Mostly she was bored with household chores and wanted to get out of the house."

Roger says he exploded, forbidding Sally to work and telling her "a mother's place is in the home." He had flatly told her, "I'll take care of the bills—you take care of the kids and the house."

Roger shakingly hands over a letter his wife left before she "tiptoed" out of the house that morning. In the letter Sally says, "I feel so trapped, so unappreciated, so tired of it all. I just end up cleaning the same dirty things over and over again—dirty dishes, dirty clothes, dirty bathroom! I just can't stand it! Life is too short and I'm not wasting any more of it. I love you and the kids, but I'll suffocate if I don't get away. I've tried to tell you this a hundred times, but you just wouldn't listen!!! I just can't be like your mother and stay at home and wait on the family like she did. I'd go crazy! As it is, I feel like I'm just going to shrivel up and die! Don't try to find me. Give me some space. I'll be in touch when I can begin to think straight again."

This case is typical of an inattentive husband who is busy at his own job and has little appreciation for the homemaker's job. While Roger gets bonuses and promotions for his work, Sally gets no medals! She faces household jobs that are neverending. There is little sense of accomplishment in dusting or ironing or cleaning the refrigerator. Sally might have found some friends in her neighborhood if she had tried, but that's not always easy when most of the wives work. She feels isolated, unappreciated, and trapped.

Sally was a secretary before she married, and she hopes it may not be too late for her to brush up on her typing and bookkeeping skills. Part of her problem is low self-esteem. She really doesn't know if she can compete out in the world, and she feels as though this may be her last opportunity to try.

Roger's understanding of male-female roles restricts Sally from employment outside the home and limits her sense of accomplishment. Sally's awareness of other models for marriage has been heightened by her neighbors' lifestyles. When Roger wouldn't change his stance, she finally made a decision to leave.

The pastor can listen and console Roger in his grief and pain. Roger very quickly will need to make adjustments in his working hours or hire a sitter to watch his daughter all day and his son before and after school. The pastor can perhaps help Roger locate care for his children, at least until the crisis passes. Efforts could be made to locate Sally and encourage her to come for counseling. If she is open to that idea, issues to be addressed include the problem of Sally's loneliness, low self-esteem and boredom, and Roger's beliefs regarding marriage roles and the form of governance at home. If he would be open to a more participatory form of family decision-making and consider some of Sally's concerns regarding self-fulfillment, this relationship might have a chance of survival.

Often, however, women like Sally have given up on making changes in the family system and never return home permanently. Many eventually remarry men who are more tolerant of a wife working outside the home. In such a case, the primary focus of counseling will be upon Roger to help him adapt to a single-parent lifestyle.

In recent years, Christian counselors frequently encounter conservative Christians who have a very strong concept of headship in the home. This view has often been "baptized" as the only Christian pattern for marital relationships (largely based on Ephesians 5). But within that same chapter is a model of mutual submission to one another which gives us a partnership form of government as an alternative "Christian" model for marriage. The reality is that the "Father Knows Best" kind of family (Dad goes to work, Mom stays home with one or more children) is found in fewer and fewer households. Even with the significant costs of day care, more and more couples have agreed that both spouses working full time is the only way they'll be able to afford a home of their own in the suburbs. This means that in many communities, the lonely, depressed stay-at-home wife has few neighbors with whom to share her concerns. She's more likely to spend her days with soap operas where crises are abundant but manageable, or romance novels where passion reigns on every page! It's a hard act for a husband to follow!

MIKE AND RUTH: PRESSURE-FILLED PASTORAL MARRIAGE

Mike and Ruth have been involved in a pastoral ministry in the Midwest for the past twelve years. The district superintendent receives a call on a Monday morning from the board chairman of First Church where Mike pastors. The chairman relates that there are serious problems between the pastor and his wife which have been devastating to the church. On Sunday evening Pastor Mike read a two-line resignation letter to the church, stating he was leaving his wife and leaving the church, effective immediately. With no explanation other than that, he closed the service (before it had really begun), left the church and drove away. The church was stunned. Several of the members are terribly concerned for Ruth's emotional state. Sunday night she was shocked and speechless.

The board chairman requests that the district superintendent drive over as soon as possible, since Ruth is hysterical with grief. The district superintendent quickly cancels his appointments and, accompanied by his wife, drives the two hours to First Church to see Ruth.

Upon reaching the parsonage, they are greeted at the door by Ruth, still in her bathrobe, looking uncharacteristically unkempt. She immediately begins to weep and has to be helped to the sofa to gather herself together.

Slowly a story of a stress-filled home begins to unfold. Ruth cries out, "How could Mike do such a thing to me and to the church? I don't know what I'm going to do. I'm so embarrassed, I just want to run and hide. But where would I go?"

The superintendent gently asks where Mike is and Ruth says she doesn't know for sure. She suspects he has gone to be with friends who are part of an informal encounter group which Mike started attending "to get his head together" several months back. The group was made up of some of his fellow classmates in a part-time counseling program. The superintendent almost hates to ask (but does), "Do you think there is someone else?"

71

Ruth just shakes her head and mutters, "I don't think so." The superintendent's wife asks, "Do you have any idea what caused Mike to act the way he did and resign so suddenly?"

Ruth pauses for a moment, looks into the couple's eyes to see if they can be trusted, and then begins an all too common story of problems in the parsonage. She relates that she and Mike met in Bible college and hit it off immediately. She was a gifted soloist and pianist and Mike was a talented speaker. They were "made for each other," according to Ruth. "We thought we'd make a great team in ministry." They both, however, had a nearly insatiable appetite for affirmation. The pastorate proved to be a place where they were needed and appreciated. They were always busy: Mike with preaching, teaching, counseling, administration, and committee meetings while Ruth stayed busy with choir direction, Sunday school teaching, Ladies' Mission Society, and home Bible studies.

In their early years of ministry they were pretty much to-gether, working at separate tasks but feeling involved in each other's life. Mike usually arranged his appointments so they could have lunch together. They enjoyed what they sensed was *their* ministry.

However, Mike moved to a larger church after six years and returned to school several nights a week. Ruth sensed that's when they began to drift, both away from each other emotion-ally and away from the Lord spiritually. Mike's values started to change and he, according to Ruth, was having more difficulty with some of the doctrines of the church as well as its restrictive lifestyle. Mike became increasingly irritable at home. Their sex life dwindled to nothing. Mike always seemed to have a reason to be going somewhere.

Most of this trouble had been brewing for several years, but they had hidden it pretty well from the church. Yet the schizophrenic behavior was getting to them. Ruth suggested a short leave of absence to get some marital and spiritual coun-seling. Mike wouldn't hear of it. "If the church board knew our problems, that would be the end of my career in the ministry! We would be out on the street with no job, no home, and no future."

72

Ruth said Mike was afraid it would be too hard to start over. About this same time, he began to get "a lot of strange ideas," (to use Ruth's expression) from his university classes. "He started to go to support groups that condoned all kinds of non-Christian ideas and practices, and I just lost hope that we would ever get it back together."

Ruth said Mike talked about leaving the ministry to become a professional marriage and family therapist. As she put it: "He thought he could get his own head together by figuring out other people's problems." She said he really was getting tired of living in a "glass house" and feeling like he was always being watched and judged and criticized. He felt he had to please everyone. Once several months ago he talked about doing something outlandish (such as running off to the Bahamas "to do something wild together like skinny-dipping on a nude beach and getting really drunk!"). When she expressed shock at such a fantasy, he "clammed up," and never mentioned it again.

Ruth's grief was similar to that of someone who had lost a loved one to cancer. The interminable waiting and dread were over. Now she had to do something with her own life, but she didn't know where to begin. She knew she'd have to move out of the parsonage, find an apartment and a job, and figure out her relationship to Mike.

The superintendent's focus would be on Ruth, to help her in making some of these decisions and finding a support mechanism for her in the difficult days ahead. Along with that would be an effort to get in contact with Mike. If the superintendent could locate him, he would try to persuade Mike to get marriage counseling.

I include this case study because it is all too common in the ministry. Due to the political nature of the pastor's life, it is difficult for pastors and their wives to be candid regarding their problems. According to Mary LaGrand Bouma's book, *Divorce in the Parsonage*, many pastors and wives don't have a single close friend.[5] When pastoral couples try to be intimate with a particular family in the church, it is often perceived as showing favoritism. Churches often expect their clergy couples to be models of perfection and forget their human component.

Several things could have halted the slide down this destructive spiral in which Mike and Ruth found themselves. First, every pastor and his wife should have someone (a former classmate or a colleague) who serves as a pastor to them. Second, vocational counseling and marriage-enrichment programs should be required periodically for all pastors and spouses. Third, retreats (possibly for three or four days per quarter) need to be set aside for the pastor and his wife to get away from the pressures of ministry to get a sense of the direction they're going. If, as in the case of Mike and Ruth, the relationship is seriously jeopardized, some marital and vocational counseling should be made available.

GENERAL OBSERVATIONS

Several important themes run throughout these case studies: loneliness, incompatibility, stress, low self-esteem, and role problems. Every case study dealt with some aspect of *isolation* and *loneliness.* Such feelings make people very vulnerable to temptation and destructive behavior. Particularly, the church needs to take a new look at its women's ministries as they apply to both homemaker and career woman. Both struggle in their own ways with feeling isolated and alone. Dobson asks,

> Did the farmer of 100 years ago come in from the fields and say, "Tell me how it went with the kids today?" . . . The difference . . . is a breakdown in the relationship between women! A century ago, women cooked together, canned together, washed clothes at the creek together, prayed together, went through menopause together, and grew old together. . . . Great emotional support was provided in this feminine contact. A woman was never alone.[6]

Dobson goes on to say, "Depriving a woman of all meaningful emotional support from outside the home puts enormous pressure on the husband-wife relationship."[7]

When my family and I arrived in Okinawa, Japan, for a three-year tour in the Navy, we experienced such stress. Cut off from friends and extended family who were thousands of miles away, my family felt isolated. Every day for two months that summer, I went off to work in a counseling center while my wife Judy and my three boys mostly waited in a hotel room. When I came "home" each evening, tired from meeting new people and learning a different job, they were ready to get out and see the sights or at least find an interesting Oriental place for dinner. Soon I felt the stress mount in all our lives. I played the rescuer of unhappy people throughout the day, and the lifter-upper of my unhappy family at night.

There was never enough of me to go around! I developed frequent chest pains for the first time in my life. I had to confront my own behavior and the subsequent stress reaction and admit that I couldn't be everything to everyone! I could not, nor was any spouse intended to, provide the total emotional support for my wife or sons or anyone else.

A woman's letter to James Dobson describes the classic "Lonely Wife." This is the way she portrays her relationship with her husband:

> He comes home late every evening. He's so tired I can actually hear his feet dragging as he approaches the porch. I look forward to his coming all day 'cause I have so much to tell him, but he doesn't feel much like talking. . . . Frankly, I like for him to talk on the telephone just so I can hear his voice. . . . Believe me, there are times when we go for a month or two without having a real, indepth conversation. . . . There's no closeness or warmth between us, yet he wants to have sex with me at the end of the day. There we are, lying in bed, having had no communication between us in weeks. He hasn't tried to be sweet or understanding or tender, yet he expects me to become passionate and responsive to him. I'll tell you, I can't do it.

And then she gets to the real point of her letter:

> We've been arguing a lot. I mean really fighting. It's the only way I can get his attention, I guess. . . . John doesn't love me anyway.[8]

She's lonely and depressed, her husband is busy and preoccupied with his work, and they just don't connect much anymore. Gone is the dating, the romance, the esteeming of each other. A generation or two ago a couple like this would probably have quietly plugged along, appearing to church friends and neighbors to be tolerably happy together. That solution has largely been abandoned. "The depressed woman can, of course, seek a divorce in the hope of starting afresh with someone more understanding and loving. Today, more than ever, this final alternative looms as the accepted method of coping with marital frustration."[9]

Another theme is *incompatibility*. As in the case of Ron and Allison, couples can make poor choices that send them down a painful road. In spite of the long-range commitment brides and bridegrooms are making, an alarmingly large number marry for all the wrong reasons: "He or she is so good looking!" or "This may be my last chance" (said already at age twenty-one or twenty-two!), or "We have such fun on dates," or "All our friends are getting married."

Lewis Smedes, in *Caring and Commitment: Learning To Live the Love We Promise*, writes about a psychologist friend who gave him a list of the most common mistakes people make when they make lifetime commitments:

> They commit too quickly.
> They commit before they are mature.
> They have unrealistic expectations.
> They commit while drunk on romantic love.
> They have a wretched self-image.
> They don't know how to communicate.
> They don't share the same faith or values.[10]

Smedes argues that a poor choice of partner doesn't have to mean the end of the marriage. It does mean that spouses have to work harder at the relationship. He goes on to say,

> A mistake at the start does not have to mean failure at the finish. None of us marries the perfect person for us; to be honest, there is no such person. But most of us accommodate

ourselves to the less-than-perfect person we did marry, even if we were not seeing straight when we married him—or her. Often when two people decide that they married the wrong person, they are really refusing to let each other be the special individuals they are. They hold the thoroughly wrong-headed notion that two committed people ought to be totally alike. And they believe that if people remain very different from each other, they have cause to split.[11]

Smedes concludes by saying, "The only way to keep commitments to people, sometimes, is by indulging their failings, accommodating to their limits, and waiting out their neuroses. Because caring is the business of commitment."[12]

The issue of *stress* as a marriage-killer comes back again and again. In the case of remarriage and stepfamily living, the need to succeed in the marriage puts tremendous pressure on the couple. This is also true of couples in the ministry. The very fact a pastoral couple has more to lose by getting a divorce (their job, their status, often their home) may increase the stress in their lives. Always being needed is not a blessing. It can tear into family time, personal spiritual nurturing, and marital enrichment. Many pastors' wives have half-joked that they were considering making an appointment with their husbands as a way to insure a little of their undivided attention! It's not just couples whom we counsel that need encouragement to design a life balanced by work and play. We ministers do also.

Low self-esteem, even if in only one partner, is destructive to both spouses. Many individuals live out their lives and their marriages as victims, not strong enough to fight for change, nor brave enough to reorder their world. They feel totally incapable of changing some role definitions. The one final thing they find strength to do is walking out on the marriage completely.

We have not mentioned the one component which all five cases lack, and that is love. All five representative marriages need the kind of love which is not self-serving, but which gives and cares before there is any guarantee of reciprocation. That kind of love wants to be flexible in meeting the spouse's needs for esteem and companionship.

77

Such love does not come naturally, but supernaturally. It is learned from God's Word and from being modeled by God's people. It is long on forgiveness and recognizes everyone's indebtedness. It is also honest, desiring to be "straight" with people. Such love has as its model Jesus Christ. All intervention, assessment, and treatment is aimed at developing this kind of spiritual sensitivity in couples.

The people mentioned here are typical of those found in real life situations. The patterns are universal. Because of this, a counselor can see a couple in crisis and draw some general conclusions about them and their situations. This, of course, assumes a willingness on the part of the pastor or other Christian counselor to intervene, assess, and treat those contemplating divorce or already divorced. This is an area where the church can promote a vast ministry of healing.

CHAPTER FIVE

THE PROCESS OF DIVORCE

HOW DO MARRIAGES DIE?

Death is our greatest enemy. We hate it. We fear it. We fight against it for as long as possible. On the day that I write this, a dear Christian friend passed away after months of fighting a debilitating disease. We despise the illness that could take her life. We rejoice that the disease did not conquer her spirit, which tonight is at home with the Lord.

It will not be easy for her family and friends to say good-bye to such a dear lady. Yet, we know that parting is unavoidable in this life—until the Lord comes to "make all things new."

Sadly, marriages also die, and the resulting divorce forces the same kind of gut-wrenching good-bye. It is hard to part with anything in which we have invested our very selves. We place such strong hope in our marriages at the time of the wedding. Even when many chapters of the story of our marriages have been painful and tragic, we still remember the good times— and these are hard to surrender. But sometimes sin overpowers the good in couples' lives. Then, try as we might, we cannot keep the book from ending. The marriage has died.

Divorce, a painful parting, is no less traumatic than any of the other good-byes of our lives. In fact, some counselors would tell us divorce is even more wounding than death because of the sense of failure and rejection that we feel. Divorce takes its victims through the "divorce process," a series of emotional stages, similar to death and dying.

The divorce process is a stressful time. Most people can handle one or two unusual stresses simultaneously. But when a large number of stressful events occur concurrently, it is normal to feel overwhelmed and incapable of coping. The divorcing person can feel as though he or she is facing a batting machine like the ones baseball players use to practice hitting. The machine hurls twenty or thirty balls at a standard speed and interval. As long as the interval between pitches and the speed of the pitches are reasonable, professional ballplayers can hit most of the balls. But when the speed is increased and the interval is decreased, even the Andre Dawsons and Vince Colemans can't hit the baseballs. After several late and useless swings, the batter will usually just shrug, give up, and walk away.

Marriages heading toward divorce respond the same way. Many individuals have learned how to handle numerous problems, as long as they come one at a time. But problems can be overwhelming when the speed and frequency of crises accelerate. That's when many people are tempted to give up and walk away.

Pastors and counselors can respond like good batting coaches, helping those going through the divorce process to sort out which "pitches" to "hit" (confront and deal with) and which "pitches" (hurts, insults, and slights) to ignore. We can help clients recognize what is normal in this fast-moving, emotional experience called divorce.

Paul Bohannan, professor of anthropology at Northwestern University, addresses this problem of concurrent crises in divorce:

> The complexity of divorce arises because at least six things are happening at once. They may come in a different order and with varying intensities, but there are at least six different experiences of separation. . . . I have called these six overlapping experiences (1) the emotional divorce, which centers around the problem of the deteriorating marriage; (2) the legal divorce, based on grounds; (3) the economic divorce, which deals with money and property; (4) the coparental divorce, which deals with custody, single parent homes, and visitation; (5) the community divorce, surrounding the changes of friends and community that every divorce experiences; and (6) the psychic divorce, with the problem of regaining individual autonomy.[1]

As in the baseball analogy, there is no recognizable pattern or pacing to these various crises. Clients end up facing some emotional fastballs that rocket at them in rapid-fire succession. Then, just as they are getting adjusted to these *emotional* challenges, a *legal* curve or *economic* knuckleball comes at them. It's like a change-up pitch in baseball that throws the batter off balance.

Good pastors and counselors, like good batting instructors, get to know what kinds of "pitches" couples can handle and what kinds of stresses they have never been able to cope with. The capabilities and coping skills of individuals vary. It is foolish to think that all people going through divorce have equal resiliency, endurance, and emotional strength.

SEVEN DIVORCES IN ONE

Let's look more closely at these various crises that Bohannan calls six divorces in one. To these six, I'd add a seventh, a spiritual divorce. This will be of particular concern to the pastor and the Christian counselor. Remember, these seven "divorces" are not sequential, one ending before another begins. Rather, they are a continued array of conflicts which will change as time goes on. Divorcing persons may face opposition from lawyers, employers, relatives, in-laws, or mutual friends.

Emotional Divorce. Emotional divorce is the most obvious one and the one we're most likely to think of when we hear someone is divorcing. C. S. Lewis, the late British author and Christian apologist, spoke of divorce as an emotionally traumatic event: "They (Christian churches) all regard divorce as something like cutting up a living body, as a kind of surgical operation. Some of them think the operation is so violent that it cannot be done at all; others admit it as a desperate remedy in extreme cases. They are all agreed that it is more like having both your legs cut off than it is like dissolving a business partnership or even deserting a regiment."[2]

The late Virginia Satir, renowned family therapist, has elaborated:

> Divorce is a metaphorical surgery which affects all areas of life of the individual. . . . For many people, divorce is a broken experience, and before they can go on with their lives, they need to be able to pick up the pieces. This period often includes deep emotional feelings of despair, disappointment, revenge, retaliation, hopelessness and helplessness.[3]

These emotions will, to greater or lesser degree, engulf a person from the beginning to the end of a divorce. Satir likens divorcing persons' emotional levels to those experienced by people struggling with the process of death and dying:

> At first, there is a denial of the events that have taken place and a consequent feeling of wanting to isolate oneself from the whole situation. Then anger, wherein one blames someone else for one's predicament. The third level is bargaining; a kind of situation in which one wants to look at the ledger to see that things are equal. This is often manifest over the custody of children and property settlements at the time of divorce. Then comes a period of depression, which is where much self hatred, self blame and feelings of failure

are present. Finally, after all of this, one comes to the acceptance of the situation and an acceptance of the self.[4]

I have been amazed in my work with the divorced and the divorcing at their courage in emotionally struggling through this deathlike experience. What amazes me even more is how little is written about this aspect from a Christian perspective.[5] Most books written on the subject of divorce address the ethics or the evils of divorce, with a strong effort made to save the marriages. Yet, the silence is deafening when it comes to Christians entering into the deathlike pain of those who have divorced or are being divorced. It is as if divorce is a totally rational, highly intellectual choice between biblical and existential ethics, rather than a rush of overpowering emotions which confuse and bewilder couples in crisis.

Joyce Landorf Heatherley shares these emotions regarding her marital separation in *Unworld People*. Speaking of the divorced as one type of "unworld people," she says,

> Unworld people experience their ordeal and then are shocked and stunned by the loss of friends, family and associates. There we stand, almost totally alone; and at precisely the time of our greatest need for family and friends . . . we feel abandoned. . . . The unworld tearing process seems to break down the very inner fibers of our spirit. It saps and drains us of strength or energy. Daily we encounter a new and unexpected crisis. We stumble about in a dense emotional fog and we are stunned with the unfairness of life and its unabated stream of losses. We cringe with the ever present fear that this new loss or the next blow will be the one to finish off the annihilation process. What's more, while losing friends and family you add your own paranoid thoughts and everyday craziness. Part of the daily struggle you face is the ridiculous fact that it is routinely impossible to remember even the most simple things you've done all your life. . . .[6]

If pastors or Christian counselors cannot rationally convince a couple to remain married—or in the case of couples who have already been divorced—they sometimes seem to have nothing more to say to them. A couple's divorce is viewed as a personal rejection of Christian ideas and ideals. We fail to recognize the overwhelming needs and emotions which lead to divorce. Most pastors would be deeply embarrassed and ashamed if they neglected someone whose spouse had recently died. Yet, every day, people are abandoned by the church to suffer the death of their marriage in solitude.

Very little is written by Christians concerning rehabilitation and restoration. We seem to want to remain uninvolved to avoid being tainted by the evil of divorce. Theologians, meanwhile, have decided that harsh punishment (i.e., excommunication) serves as a deterrent to other divorces. Until we decide whether punishment or rehabilitation is the church's appropriate response to divorce, we will continue to ignore its emotional pain.

The emotions of divorce are a little like a great river which at times has raging rapids and dangerous waterfalls and at other times has stagnant pools and slow-moving currents. Shock, grief, and anger are probably the strongest emotional currents in the early stages of divorce (especially for the persons being divorced).

Bruce Fisher breaks the world of divorce into "dumpers" and "dumpees" in his book *Rebuilding: When Your Relationship Ends:*[7] Dumpees' feelings include a sense of loss and grief, often attended by anger and a sense of betrayal and rejection. And Bohannan writes: "One of the reasons it feels so good to be engaged and newly married is the rewarding sensation that, out of the whole world, you have been selected. One of the reasons that divorce feels so awful is that you have been 'de-selected.' It punishes almost as much as the engagement and the wedding are rewarding."[8] The dumpee's whole sense of identity is shaken by this feeling of inadequacy. In transactional analysis language, it is the ultimate "I'm not O.K."

The dumper, on the other hand, will experience a different kind of shock and anger, combined with a significant sense of guilt. The initiator of the divorce will be shocked to discover that being divorced is not so liberating as he or she once thought. Economic problems emerge over support and legal issues; friendships are lost (or at least different), and the dating life is frightening and often shallow. Anger will grow from their own —and their spouse's—inability or unwillingness to change. Guilt arises from being the first one to give up on the relationship. The typical dumper is a Monday-morning quarterback, questioning and second-guessing motives and roles in the failed marriage.

Both dumper and dumpee carry a residual anger at being forced to make changes. They feel lonely and socially uncomfortable. After years of functioning as half of a couple, it's hard to get used to making plans and attending events alone. Plus, there is real grief for both parties over the loss of sexual intimacy, either due to enforced abstinence or a lot of superficial promiscuity.

In this phase of shock, denial, anger, and guilt, the pastor or counselor needs to listen rather than talk. Divorcing people crave affirmation. Most of all, they want to feel understood and cared for by the counselor. They may express feelings of anger or revenge that make many pastors and counselors feel uncomfortable. Pastors may be tempted to label such emotions "sin," and try to talk clients out of these feelings. They will do better to just listen and show concern. (At a later time, pastors can come back to address the self-destructiveness of these emotions.)

A pastor leading a divorce recovery group couldn't believe the group's reaction when he mentioned a newspaper item he had read. This particular group of divorcing people was *delighted* to hear about a woman who took her car and ran over her estranged husband and his girlfriend while they were picnicking in a city park. The pastor went into a long lecture on the evils of anger which led to this murder. By doing this, he not only shut down the group's energy and interest, but he failed to help the group deal with their own anger and vengefulness. By asking questions rather than preaching, the pastor/counselor could have helped individuals in the group explore their own feelings of revenge and deep resentment. He missed an opportunity to probe the group for constructive ways they had found to control and channel their own anger. This obviously could have been helpful to other group members.

Bargaining follows the initial shock, anger, and guilt of a divorce. It is normal to experience some depression as divorced people move toward acceptance. This process brings closure to the marriage emotionally. Ambivalence characterizes much of what is going on. Part of a person wants to hold on to the relationship or at least certain aspects of it; another part wants to end the marriage completely and get on with life. To complicate the issue, usually sandwiched in the middle of this phase are financial and child-custody issues. These elicit all kinds of mixed feelings regarding the spouse and a future as divorced persons who retain parenting roles.

Abigail Trafford, in her book *Crazy Time: Surviving Divorce,* addresses the problem of ambivalence:

Ambivalence is another basic stage of Crazy Time. It's the emotional mother of Doublefeel—having two contradictory feelings at once. It encompasses a wide range of emotions and serves as a psychological switching station as you swing back and forth between guilt, anger, depression and euphoria. . . . The essential nature of Crazy Time is that you can't be really sure of anything including yourself. The one thing you know is that things are going to change.[9]

The bargaining phase of the emotional divorce marks the beginning of the end of the marriage. Partners begin to acknowledge that the relationship is going to end. Last-minute attempts will be made to compromise. Some partners try to keep the marriage intact structurally, to get "half a loaf" rather than "no loaf at all." This is usually a futile gesture. Even if some bargains are struck, they usually are temporary. The basic foundation of trust and esteem are too far eroded to support the relationship.

Attempts are frequently made to resume marital intimacies, often after a long period of sexual inactivity, in an effort to cement a relationship. There are too many other emotional stressors which crack any bonding made here, so sex alone doesn't work. Couples often live apart, but date and engage in sexual relations while divorce proceedings grind on in the courts. This is one last denial of what is really happening between them.

Bargaining also involves legal issues: child custody, financial support, visitation rights, division of property. This is where the legal divorce begins, overlapping very emotional issues related to property and children. This can be a vicious stage because the future of both partners is at stake. Partners can do some healthy bargaining over these economic and support topics. But that takes great strength. Divorcing persons are asked to be empathic and flexible with partners who have either rejected them or who "drove them to divorce."

Pastors can help couples sort out their feelings here and assist them to take a middle-of-the-road course. Divorcing people need lawyers who want to facilitate a fair and amicable settlement and not prolong the proceedings for their own financial benefit. I have seen couples fight over who should get a thirty-five-dollar lamp or a two-hundred-fifty-dollar television, then spend two thousand dollars in legal fees to have their way! A pastor/counselor can be the level-headed one in the heat of this sort of conflict.

Economic and Co-parental Divorce. Layered on top of both the emotional divorce and legal divorce is the economic/co-parental divorce. Here both partners see the reality of a shared future, of children as part of the equation. Neither partner will be very well off economically. Support payments are marginal at best for the one spouse, yet significant enough to limit the lifestyle of the other. Homes and cars are often sold to split community property. Most divorcing people move down in their standard of living, into smaller quarters and older cars. Many of the luxuries go by the wayside.

This is where partners negotiate over issues of financial and emotional support of children. What part will each partner play in the upbringing and care of their children? Sadly enough, children become pawns to strike deep into the emotional territory of an ex-spouse. The reality is that children are not unfeeling pawns in this game. Pastors can help couples to affirm their children during this difficult time. Divorcing parents need to assure them that changes will take place between Mom and Dad, but that doesn't change their love for their children.

Children, too, go through a period of adjustment with similar feelings of anger, fear, sense of rejection, loss, and depression.

Divorce is a family affair and needs to be viewed from a systems perspective. To do less is to miss much of what is happening in the primary couple relationship.

One of the indicators of how the divorce process is going will be reflected in the way children handle sadness, anger, aggression, and self-esteem. If there is a lot of aggressive acting out or depressive suicidal behavior, it is a good indicator that the divorce is slow in arriving at resolution. It is common for children to fantasize that their parents will get back together. They may even make attempts to bring this about.[10]

The church has remained deathly silent in regard to ministering to these hurting families. Even if some parental behavior is disdained, we have a responsibility to help children get through their parents' divorce emotionally and spiritually healthy. We may find it hard to communicate to children that they are accepted if we remain aloof to parents in pain. But that leaves us in danger of violating Jesus' mandate: "Let the little children come to me, and do not hinder them, for the Kingdom of Heaven belongs to such as these" (Matt. 19:14 NIV).

Once the bargaining is over, with a general resolution of legal, economic, and child-custody issues (but prior to a final court appearance), there is often a period of depression. A divorcing person awakens to the fact that the marriage really is over and he or she now must struggle to accept that fact. This is a self-critical time; partners implode a lot of anger. Suicidal ideas and gestures are common, along with significant drug and alcohol abuse. If an intervention is not forthcoming, self-destructive, even fatal, habits can be acquired.

Pastors and counselors can help individuals to accept change and renew their hope in the future. Cognitive-behavior therapy that examines negative thinking and changes self-image may be in order. Obviously, chemical dependency and suicidal behavior must be challenged.

Community Divorce. Layered over these emotional issues is the community divorce. Friends, relatives, co-workers, and fellow church members recognize that the marriage is actually going to end. Up to this point, they have been hoping it wouldn't come to this, not just for the couple's sake, but for their own sake. Insightful people recognize that their relationship with the divorced couple will change. Some of these changes will require adjustments by friends and family as well as by the divorcing couple. Some friends may be fearful that divorce is contagious and their marriages may be threatened. Relatives and friends may have to choose sides. Sometimes in-laws are cut off from sons-in-law and daughters-in-law whom they have come to love. Even if there's no special closeness with the daughter-in-law or son-in-law, grandparents know their relationships with grandchildren may change.

Certain employee-employer relationships change, particularly for couples in Christian ministry where loss of vocation occurs at the same time as the emotional loss of a spouse. For this reason, the price of marital failure for clergy couples is considerably higher than that of almost any other profession. Divorce takes its toll economically, emotionally, and spiritually when it destroys ministry. Divorcing pastors receive little or no communal support. This makes long-term recovery much more uncertain. In contrast, the average church member, at least, can continue to practice his or her vocation after divorce.[11]

Psychic Divorce. Emotionally, this is the last stage, when acceptance is finally reached, often referred to as the psychic divorce. Divorcing persons come to peace with "what is," forsaking a lot of "what was" and "what could have been." This is a burial time for the marriage. However, ex-spouses don't forget the past; they can mentally revisit scenes of their marriage. Only gradually does the focus shift to new interests. This may take place at the courthouse or a few weeks to several months after all legal proceedings have ceased.

Often one ex-spouse reaches this stage before the other. One partner will still try to keep things alive while the other is focused on a new life. When the non-custodial parent visits his or her children, the ex-spouse may neurotically try to monitor childcare methods or social life. Sometimes, only the passage of time or the relocation of the family terminates this behavior. A good pastor understands that changes are difficult—but necessary.

Spiritual Divorce. This leads to the final phase in the death of a marriage (the one pastors will definitely want to address), the spiritual aspect of divorce. How do we help clients rebuild their inner spiritual life? In my workbook, *Recovering From Divorce*, I outline some specific steps to make this happen for divorced couples. This involves learning from the past, dealing with the present, and planning for the future with an eye to God's grace and guidance.[12]

Crucial to recovery is a basic understanding of repentance and forgiveness before God and man. If divorce is viewed as sin, each partner needs to seek God's pardon for his or her part in the failure of the marriage. One reason divorced persons can't forgive ex-spouses is because they find it difficult to claim God's forgiveness for themselves. They are continually counting transgressions to see who is the greater sinner, self or spouse. They forget we all have sinned and fail at times in human relationships.

Other clients steeped in guilt need to read Psalm 51 and Psalm 103 to grasp the breadth of God's grace. King David was an adulterer and murderer who was later known as a man "after the heart of God." We need to read how Jesus dealt with the woman caught in adultery in John 8, to understand his attitude toward human failure and sin.

Jim Smoke's book *Growing Through Divorce* has an excellent chapter on finding and experiencing forgiveness. He says, "Experiencing forgiveness gets the hate out of your life permanently."[13] This is not magic. Rather, it is a process which takes place only when we realize that we also are debtors who need forgiveness. Once we receive forgiveness, we can become generous and offer it to others.

Most people who fail at marriage take one of two extreme positions: They either have an unrepentant heart, or they are so burdened with guilt or anger that they cannot grasp God's grace. A counselor needs to remind the insensitive one of God's judgment of sin. Meanwhile, he or she needs to remind the guilt-ridden one of God's love and acceptance. Both need God's forgiveness: One with the tough discipline of the law, the other with the gentle wooing of God's grace.

The pastor and counselor should recognize the stages of divorce and be willing to walk beside those in deep pain. That doesn't mean that we don't share our ethical as well as practical concerns in the midst of the process. But our care and counsel must be sensitive to the emotional and spiritual development of individuals. We need to be creative in recognizing nurturing moments when our encouragement and instruction will be appropriate and accepted. Sometimes, we're just called to lovingly listen to the pain of those who have parted.

Jason Towner best captures the painful farewell to his marriage and the grief process that follows:

> I did not stand at a casket or graveside to say good-bye to Jane. But, our farewell was just as final. I said good-bye to the person and ten months later to the memory. I looked around for a brief moment. Then I turned out the light, pulled the door shut, heard it lock, and slowly walked up the corridor that would lead to my healing. Jane now occupies a quiet place in my heart.[14]

Divorce is made up of a number of simultaneous events which can so overwhelm the divorcing persons that they cannot possibly imagine life after divorce. Those who have worked with the divorced and divorcing know that the joy in living can—and does—return after days and weeks of mourning. Counselors must dare to enter into this process with those who are experiencing the death of their marriages. Divorcing people may again experience the joy of salvation and an abundant life in Christ.

CHAPTER SIX

THE PERSON WHO INTERVENES

WHAT IS THE PASTOR'S OR COUNSELOR'S ROLE?

My mother, bless her soul, was proud of her son being in the ministry. However, that didn't stop her from pointing out to me one day, "David, do you realize the first wedding you performed was for a marriage that lasted three weeks?" And I had to admit that had already been brought to my attention. As a fledgling pastor, twenty-four-years old, I was tempted never to officiate at another wedding for fear of failure.

But, in the almost twenty years since then, I've decided the failure of that marriage was not *my* failure—unless I had neglected premarital counseling and personal care for that couple, and I hadn't. I had simply been pressured into performing that wedding by influential church members. I had had serious doubts about the couple's ability to establish a Christian marriage, but the bride's mother, our Sunday school superintendent, didn't want to hear any of my concerns. She went ahead and planned a wedding which I was expected to perform. My failure, then, was in bowing to her wishes against my better judgment.

Three weeks later, that bride ran off with a man with whom she worked. I was left to comfort a stunned and disillusioned bridegroom. I was nearly overwhelmed by the task of walking with someone through the pain of separation and, in this case, divorce. If I'd had a choice, I would have probably referred him to a professional counselor. But Jack made it clear that I was the pastor who knew him and could best minister to him in this crisis.

This points out the special role pastors play when members of their congregations turn to them in times of crisis, when they need a familiar caregiver, a friend, who is trained as both a pastor and a counselor. Another part of this special relationship involves prevention of, as well as response to, marital crises. What can the pastor do to promote healthy marriages, and how does he or she intervene in dysfunctional relationships? I see this pastoral role as having three components: The pastor as a generalist, the pastor as a specialist, and the pastor as a person.

THE PASTOR AS A GENERALIST

When we think about a generalist in the pastoral ministry, we envision an old country parson, marrying, baptizing, and burying the faithful. The imagery is of a loving and caring person who is much like Marcus Welby, M.D., the television character of a few years back. Remember how the general practitioner took time for the ordinary concerns of his patients' lives? Only when problems became too technical for him (and that was not often) did he refer his people to the more impersonal specialists.

When we talk about pastors as generalists, we see them observing, facilitating, praying, interpreting, preaching, and modeling.

The Pastor Observes

The pastor is in a unique position to be an observer. He or she visits homes, attends church and community social events, and works on committees with his people. It doesn't take long to notice patterns of conflict, areas of neglect, and negative attitudes.

In short, the observant pastor can see trouble coming long before it explodes destructively in people's lives. Some of the things we may ask ourselves are obvious: *How does this couple or family communicate? Is there a lot of shouting? When? At whom? Who gets interrupted? By whom? Who sits close to whom at church?*

And some of the things the pastor will be wondering about are more subtle: *Who seems to need more attention than they receive? Who's in charge of this household? Are the children acting out difficulties between the parents? What is the level of spiritual life in this home?*

Recently one of my sons had a teenage friend over watching a late-night football game. The boy's father came to pick up his son just as the game went into overtime. The boy stayed glued to the television, ignoring his father, who first called for him and then waited outside in his car. Only upon my strong suggestion that he not keep his father waiting any longer did the boy finally get up to go. That boy's disrespectful behavior gave me some indication of a strained father-son relationship. A pastor observes situations similar to this every day and makes plans to intervene and help.

The Pastor Facilitates

The pastor is a facilitator of community. Often the pastor provides the connecting link between the families in the church. I remember as a young pastor the frustration my wife and I felt that so few families seemed able to relate to one another directly. They all preferred to make me the link that connected them. Yet, several years later, we enjoyed fellowship in a church where a number of social and spiritual gatherings succeeded in bringing families together—with or without the pastor. What made the difference?

The pastor of that warm and caring church was, himself, loving and concerned for people. But he had been in ministry long enough to recognize that sometimes certain social, educational, and economic barriers could not be overlooked, at least not without his personal charisma and presence. As facilitators, pastors will function as matchmakers, attempting to connect individuals and families around common backgrounds and interests. Marriages are strengthened as Christian families fellowship together. Conflicts between spouses are more manageable when they can be shared and prayed about with close church friends.

We share a common bond as members of the same Body. But often we're more comfortable with people with similar histories, or training, or leisure-time activities. The pastor will try harder to have such people meet and then let those people share their own stories. Pastors and spouses, themselves, can profit from one or more close relationships like this.

The Pastor Prays

The pastor is an intercessor. This may be the most neglected aspect of pastoral care and counseling. Few texts on pastoral life do more than touch on this issue; but it is the most powerful intervention strategy of all.

Prayer is an essential part of Christian counseling. Richard Foster in his book, *Money, Sex and Power,* addresses this type of spiritual leadership by pastors:

> How do spiritual leaders serve their people? They serve them by learning the ways of prayer. People desperately need the ministry of prayer. Marriages are being shattered. Children are being destroyed. People are living in dark depression and misery. We can make a difference if we will learn to pray. If we genuinely love people, we will desire for them far more than it is within our power to give them, and that will lead us to prayer. . . . One caution: We must pray for people in the utmost simplicity and joy. We do not try to psychoanalyze them or to figure everything out. We do not even try to correct their theology. We simply invite the Lord to enter the mind and heart and to heal them both and to restore the God-intended personality.[1]

When it comes to prayer for healing, either physical or emotional, many pastoral counselors aren't sure of themselves—or of God's power. Foster offers this encouragement:

95

Your people expect you to bring the ministry of healing prayer. When you go into a home and see people bowed low with the sorrows of life, it is the most natural thing in the world to lay your hands upon them in the sacramental way and pray for their wholeness. . . . We do not need to be frightened of the few times when no improvement is noticeable, for there are many other times when much good has been done.[2]

The Pastor Interprets

The pastor is an interpreter of the Word every Sunday from the pulpit—and every day by the example of his or her own life. When pastors are willing to share their own struggles and weaknesses, they show the true relevance of Scripture to modern-day living. Pastors offer guidance for living, grace for failure, love for relationships, and meaning for the searching of their people. Such interpretations involve a balance between study and visitation: Spending enough time studying the Word and meditating to sense God's will, and then spending enough time in the world, attempting to understand the issues which challenge people's lives. By the very nature of the word "interpret," we bridge two worlds, sharing what God has declared in his Word with how people live their lives. There, obviously, is an instructional quality to this ministry. But it is more like an athletic coach working with athletes than a professor lecturing students.

Pastors stand with one foot in the Word and the other in the world. Perhaps that's why it's difficult to maintain a balance between the two. We've all known pastors who spend nearly all their time in their office, door closed, phone off the hook, studying. But we've also known preachers who can most often be found at the local coffee shop or at someone's home.

The task of interpreter is not an easy one. The pastor tries to share spiritual reality with a world which denies its existence. When it comes to marriage and divorce, the pastor wants to make people aware of God's standards for holiness and faithfulness. The pastor also wants people to know the power of the Holy Spirit to enable them to live with an imperfect spouse.

The Pastor Preaches

Everyone recognizes the pastor as preacher. Hurting people listen especially for themes of love, grace, faithfulness, forgiveness, holiness, and healing. A parishioner's view of God is determined by these messages. So the pastor has the opportunity to shape people's beliefs not only about God, but about themselves, too, depending on the kinds of sermons they hear week after week. Pastors need to make the plan of salvation clear to those who are still outside God's family.

The limitations of preaching lie in the willingness—or unwillingness—of listeners to act upon revealed truth. Henry Davis, in *Design for Preaching*, states:

> Nothing is more futile than an exhortation to persons who are not ready to act on it, nothing more hopeless than the attempt to reassure persons in a situation that does not justify reassurance. . . . A person who has not taken and will not take any of the basic steps toward becoming a Christian is not ripe for true Christian exhortation or any form of Christian therapy.[3]

If a Christian is open to God's leading in his or her life, preaching and counseling can be therapeutic and life-changing. If a person is unwilling to surrender his or her will to God, no amount of preaching (or therapy) will change the situation. This is especially true in regard to the divorced and the divorcing. The role of pastor as preacher can be used mightily to bring healing and wholeness to those who are open to God's will and way.

The Pastor Models

The pastor models the Christian life before the people: love, joy, peace, patience, kindness, goodness, faithfulness, gentleness, and self-control (Gal. 5:23 NIV). These attributes are revealed in one's relationships with church members, with one's spouse and children, and with God. They are even more evident when there are disagreements and conflicts involving the pastor. The black church has an expression: A man of God must not only "talk the talk, but walk the walk."

There is a genuine need for people who can demonstrate, through every aspect of their own lives, a style of relationship that is pleasing to God. As John Stott says in his book, *Between Two Worlds,* "People will no more accept our Christian message if our life contradicts it than they would take a cold cure recommended by a salesman who coughs and sneezes between each sentence."[4] There are so few models of Christian living and Christian marriage which are worth imitating. Perhaps it is because such exemplary living comes only through the Person and the power of the Holy Spirit.

THE PASTOR AS A SPECIALIST

Pastors play a very special role as counselors. They may not be trained therapists; they may not even identify any particular counseling skills they possess. But they are often the first people called to intervene in crisis situations.

Pastors Do Crisis Counseling

Families call pastors when a church member is told he or she has cancer. Couples call late at night for pastors to intervene in dangerous family fights. The pastor is called to bring comfort when a child is injured or killed in a traffic accident. Pastors are called to nursing homes where senior citizens have been abandoned by their families. The pastor frequently deals with problems arising from drug and alcohol addiction. Pastors sometimes find themselves trying to bring safety and sanity to the violence of spouse-abuse and child-abuse incidents. Occasionally, pastors are confronted with suicide, unwanted pregnancies, abortions, and teenage runaways. Whether they like it or not, much of the pain and brokenness of the world ends up on their doorstep. And amazingly, most pastors handle this challenging, front-line duty very well!

Pastors Do Marriage Enrichment

A lot of preventive care for marriages is given by pastors in premarital counseling and marriage-enrichment programs. These focus on family life-cycle issues, communication-skill development, and spiritual renewal. Families need pastoral help if they are going to survive the pressures of contemporary society. According to a study of returnees to the church, "Forty-five to 55 per cent say they return or convert to the church because they need help with their family life. That is the number one reason given for converting to or returning to the church."[5]

Pastors Do Marriage Counseling

Pastors may be the first to observe a certain "drift" in people's lives and marriages when problems are still small and manageable. The pastor may start a conversation with a question: "I wonder if you're doing O.K.—or has something got you down?"

The rituals of attachment—locating, tracking with one's eyes and ears, reaching out to, touching, holding, caressing —have been replaced by an almost opposite set of rituals— not knowing where the other is, withdrawing from bodily contact, pushing the other away, striking in rage, avoiding the sight and sound of the other. In public, these signs of separation can be noted even by strangers, but especially by an observant pastor.[6]

A pastor may decide marriage counseling would be beneficial to such a couple, but sometimes spouses are reluctant to begin. Men, especially, may actually fear counseling. One man described marriage counseling this way:

Keeping an appointment with a marriage counselor is the nearest a man will ever come to visiting a gynecologist. If a marriage counselor is to help, you have to become naked about your life, your marriage, your sexuality. The counselor will probe and the probing will be uncomfortable. Some men adamantly refuse the treatment that can bring healing.[7]

A pastor can usually persuade a husband to come in for an evaluation if the pastor has had a positive relationship with the man prior to the crisis situation. Often a pragmatic approach is helpful, underlining that there is little joy in the relationship presently; and with a little hard work they may be able to get their marriage on track. I have encouraged men to do themselves a favor before doing something rash. They can check out their troubled relationship to see the extent of work that is needed in order to repair it. To do anything else beforehand is premature. Two more suggestions may help: 1) Pastors can briefly state their qualifications to counsel marriage partners, and 2) pastors can assure couples that what they reveal in counseling will be held in the strictest confidence. And obviously, the pastor needs a reputation for upholding that promise.

A counselor is a little like an auto mechanic. When you have something wrong under the hood of your car and it begins making weird noises, you don't pull off the road and destroy the car. Instead, you haul it into a garage and have it put on a lube rack. The mechanic analyzes the problem. It may be something as minor as corroded spark plugs or a loosened hose. Or it might be a major calamity, like a cracked piston or a nonfunctioning transmission.

After analyzing the problem, the counselor, like a mechanic, describes the seriousness of the conflict. Once the couple knows the extent of their problem, they must decide whether they want to pay the emotional price to have their marriage repaired. If the couple is motivated to work on their problems and resolve their conflicts, I usually ask them to agree to a six-session counseling format.

First, I attempt to get a good relational history, identify problem areas, and deal with goals, values, and communication styles. I then try to see how flexible the couple is to change. If they are rigid and inflexible, counseling will be a waste of time. We might as well terminate it.

Howard Clinebell shares his pastoral counseling strategy in the following steps: "Identifying the pain, becoming aware of surviving satisfactions and strengths, stating your [client's] needs clearly and directly, and re-contracting to meet more of each person's needs."[8]

As a pastor, I want to know what threatens each individual's psychic survival. Because I'm dealing with two unique individuals, one male and one female, I can't assume they have the same or even similar needs. Even spouses may not be aware of their partner's specific needs or desires, or how much they differ from their own.

Lewis Smedes lists four basic human needs which can overwhelm people emotionally:

1. Survival needs: What we need to keep body and spirit together.
2. Moral needs: What we need to keep a sense of our personal integrity.
3. Power needs: What we need to take responsibility for our own lives.
4. Spiritual needs: What we need to relate to God in gratitude and love.

There comes a time in every committed relationship when one person has to give up what he wants so that the other person can get what she needs. But he should not give up what he needs so that the other person can get whatever she wants. . . .

The trick is knowing the difference between our needs and our desires.[9]

Smedes gives some basic ground rules for settling conflicts between needs and desires. He maintains that desires should always give way to needs, not the reverse. He believes both desires and needs are negotiable: "If getting what I want prevents you from getting what you want, we negotiate; neither of us surrenders, both of us compromise. . . . If getting what I need prevents you from getting what you need, we negotiate as equals, from strength to strength; we compromise our less basic needs so that both of us can meet our more basic needs."[10]

Even in my own relationships, my background as a U.S. Navy chaplain serving with the Marines sometimes leads me to ask myself, "Is this a hill worth dying on?" I encourage couples to fight for an important need or value and let pass the less important conflicts. Some issues just aren't worth the time or emotion.

Pastors and counselors often encounter people who have irrational or destructive beliefs about themselves, their spouse, or their world. This might be a good time to use "cognitive restructuring," a form of counseling that deals with harmful thought patterns and unrealistic expectations. Howard Stone observes, in *Using Behavioral Methods in Pastoral Counseling*, that "changing unconstructive belief systems is not easy. It requires considerable counseling finesse. Yet ministers, because of their training in both counseling and belief systems, are in an ideal position among all the helping professionals for enabling people to rid themselves of irrational ideas."[11]

Yet pastors are sometimes at a loss to know just how to proceed in the counseling process. Lawrence Brammer, in *The Helping Relationship: Process and Skills*, describes the steps of the counseling plan as he sees them: In Phase One, "Building Relationships," he includes entry, clarification, structure (formulating the contract), and relationship. His Phase Two, "Facilitating Positive Action," involves exploration, consolidation (exploring alternatives, working through feelings, practicing new skills), planning, and termination.[12]

The pastor's role in this process is to get the couple talking. But then the counselor needs to step back and let the couple do just that—talk to each other. This leads the partners to feel *they*, not the pastor, are responsible for changes in their marriage. Meanwhile, pastors listen and observe communication patterns: Who talks to whom? In what tone? What do they actually say? (Is there illogical thinking? Unrealistic expectations, etc.?) A pastor will begin to get a sense of a couple's spirituality. Suggestions will be offered when the pastor thinks the couple will receive them and try to apply them—and not before.

Couples can be taught ways of dealing with their problems. Some counselors make use of a lot of homework. It is one way for couples to show their diligence in working out conflicts. Others use role reversal to get spouses to experience how their partner feels about an issue. Role playing is also used to help people understand how others view them. Other pastors and counselors use imagery to help a couple project themselves into a different setting (perhaps back to a previous, happier occasion). This is often useful in rekindling warm feelings for the spouse.

Pastors will also want to use Scripture in their counseling. For example, when a couple reflects on their anger or guilt over adultery, the pastor can tell the story of David and Bathsheba (from 2 Samuel 11 and 12). When a couple complains that they are losing their identity, the pastor can refer to Jesus' words, "For whoever wants to save his life, will lose it; but whoever loses his life for me will find it" (Matt. 16:25 NIV).

Pastors and Christian counselors realize no human techniques have power to transform lives. Only the Holy Spirit can do that!

What circumstances indicate to the pastor that it is useless to work on saving the marriage? Successful counseling is really contingent on the old adage, "You can lead a horse to water, but you can't make him drink." Each partner must have the motivation and support to resolve critical or chronic problems; otherwise, marital therapy is a futile exercise. Spouses may have divergent values and goals. This, in itself, should not preclude counseling. The issue that needs to be determined is, "How elastic is this relationship?"

Another complicating issue is the intensity of subversion or violence within blended families. Is it possible to get the couple to unite and face sabotaging efforts by children or extended family? Some couples may opt to end the relationship rather than risk losing their sons, daughters, and parents (particularly if suicide gestures, delinquent behavior, family violence, or runaway episodes increase in frequency and intensity). It takes a particularly strong couple to face intense intimidation of this type. Their involvement in a stepparent support group is essential.

The pastor, then, takes a number of these factors into consideration when deciding whether to refer couples for couples therapy. Francine Klagsbrun describes those who have the greatest likelihood of success:

Who, then, can benefit from therapy? Couples who care deeply about one another, but can't seem to get along; couples who have become overwhelmed by problems between them that they can no longer solve themselves; couples engulfed by tragedies—a job loss, a death in the family, an illness—who need support in coping; couples so caught up in anger and depression that they have forgotten the roots of their relationship, the reason they married in the first place, and want to rediscover those roots; couples who fight recurrent battles, rehashing the same issues again and again without being able to move on, to accept the differences between them or simply live with those differences.[13]

Throughout their conflicts, the couple has a sense of being "stuck." The pressures on the marriage may have an external or internal source; regardless, there is a determination to fix things one way or another. Therapy can be helpful in providing insight into negative relational patterns. It can improve communication, deal with fantasy, illusion, and mind reading. It also can help partners come to grips with problems in their family history.

Therapists generally regard therapy as successful if they can help a couple end a marriage which they seem unable to end themselves. Obviously, this goal is not often shared by clergy. In their eyes, such an outcome is tantamount to admitting defeat and failure. Therapists, on the other hand, see people caught in increasingly destructive cycles and have a hard time justifying retention of the marriage relationship at any cost.

Klagsbrun lists several things marital counseling cannot do: "(1) Make over one partner to suit the ideals of the other. (2) Become a substitute for honesty in marriage. (3) Substitute for dealing with issues in a couple's own home and lives. (4) Resurrect a marriage that is already dead, by lack of participation by one partner."[14]

THE PASTOR AS A PERSON

The pastor as a person is crucial to ministry to the divorced and divorcing. If a pastor's life is not in order, he is subject to all sorts of temptations in marital counseling and community ministry. The church has been scandalized enough with the sexual adventures of a number of well-known clergy.

Pastors know they need to nurture their own marriage and family life, but sometimes these needs are overlooked. Ministers genuinely want to feel needed. So easily, male pastors can become entrapped in affairs with women seeking empathy and counsel from clergy. Pastors appear to be so understanding and supportive to conflict-ridden women who don't feel listened to at home. The subsequent transference dynamic can quickly get out of hand, especially if the pastor's wife is not very affirming or affectionate.

Other stressors also find their way into a pastor's life: an unreasonable job description, poor pay, long work hours (often out of sequence to family leisure time), high visibility, and inadequate management training. Pastors need to guard their time to ensure personal growth and spiritual nurture. They also need to recharge their energies by spending relational time with family or friends outside of the church. If these basic needs are neglected, the minister is in danger of burnout or moral shipwreck.

I have a pastor friend who negotiated a long weekend (Thursday to Monday) once a quarter, in addition to his annual vacation, so he and his wife could refocus on their marriage and ministry. Though it cost the church the extra expense of a guest speaker once a quarter, the plan paid large dividends. Not only were goals kept realistic, but the pastoral couple were able to do the kind of preventive work on their own relationship that refreshed them to minister with new energy and vision. Because of the high stress environment of the church, it is important that such steps be taken to insure a long-tenured, stable ministry team.

Finally, the pastor must take care of his own spirit. That means immersion in the Word of God to be able to instinctively respond to situations based upon scriptural principles. It involves the life of prayer, where God works in our heart and the hearts of those we pray for, to bring about his glory.

If pastors learn anything in the experience of "moving up" to larger churches or responsibilities, it is that the inner life is constantly being attacked by the urgent demands of life and ministry. Twenty years from now, most of those issues will not be remembered. A pastor must guard his or her heart or there will be no heart to share with others! If we are going to have anything to say authoritatively to people struggling with their marriages, it must come from a life and marriage which models the love of God, full of forgiveness and faith. We cannot legitimately call people to live a life that we have found impossible to live ourselves. But we can demonstrate God's love is at work in our world and in our own marriage.

The pastor plays a significant role in intervening in the lives of the divorced and divorcing. We need to live faithfully to expect faith in our people; to live lovingly to expect love in our people; to live righteously to expect righteousness in our people.

CHAPTER SEVEN

THE CONTEXT OF DIVORCE

WHERE IS A LOVING COMMUNITY?

When I was growing up in the 1950s, I remember a feeling of connectedness and belonging among neighbors and church friends. I have several snapshots in my mental scrapbook of those days: pictures of neighbors helping each other bale hay; of women bringing casseroles to a home where the mother was ill or a family member had died; of friends sitting on our front porch after Sunday dinner to share animated conversation about our faith, or sharing stories of "the good ol' days." We cared for each other, and shared values and purposes. We felt knit together—like family.

When emotional storms hit us, we didn't carry the burden alone. At age fifteen, when my father suffered a heart attack, the community of faith gathered around to support our family. Shortly after my father was hospitalized that December, our well froze solid. We were left without water and with no money to hire a repairman to come and thaw out the pipes. So, from December until May, when warm spring weather finally thawed out that well, an elder from our church drove ten miles out of his way every day to bring twenty gallons of water to our home. He put feet to his faith and lived out a life of love before the watching eyes of a teenage boy yet undecided about the Christian life.

Midway through that spring, my father had a second heart attack and died. In the grief-stricken days that followed, my heart was filled with fear and sorrow. Several weeks following that heart-rending event, another elder knocked on my door at five o'clock on a Saturday morning to take me fishing. Throughout that whole summer, he faithfully appeared early each Saturday, convincing me he needed a fishing partner. Now I realize he was really there sharing that bucket of minnows and a boat filled with tackle on a Wisconsin lake to lovingly listen to my anger, pain, and confusion.

These men were not psychologists or pastors. They were just two Christian laymen—a mink rancher and a railroad switchman. They loved me into the Kingdom and helped me through a very painful time in my life.

This is the kind of loving concern, motivated by the love of God, that the apostle James describes: "Religion that God our Father accepts as pure and faultless is this: To look after orphans and widows in their distress and to keep oneself from being polluted by the world" (James 1:27 NIV). Where is this kind of ministry today among the many single-parent homes in our neighborhoods?

CHANGING TIMES

Much of this sense of community is gone in our fast-paced urban society. The lack of concern and support for our neighbor has stripped the American family of critical resources in troubled times. We feel alone. Who is there to share problems with before they become compound, complex, and critical? I believe the lack of deep, informal peer relationships is a significant factor in the breakdown of the family, and of divorce, in particular.

Communities began to change with the industrialization and urbanization of the late 1800s when people left farms and rural areas for work in factories and cities. Typical American families became very mobile, relocating several times in search of a better life. Often these moves were cross-continental, moving families far from relatives and friends.

My family lived throughout my entire youth and adolescence in the same town, near the same neighbors. Furthermore, these were people who shared most of my family's views and values. But in the thirty-some years since then, social changes and a modern, mobile lifestyle have placed people with a variety of world views next door. Any consensual outlook on the world has dissipated. Relativism and pluralism have allowed diverse people to live close to one another with minimal conflicts. When differences with one's neighbors were unresolvable, a move to another state or region was not so difficult. People who wanted to could always find a place to live in anonymity.

In short, the glue of shared values, especially Christian values, no longer holds communities together. The adhesive of Christian consensus has been ripped away, resulting in a loss of commitment and accountability to one another. Individuals find themselves lonely and isolated in their neighborhoods, jobs, even in their churches. Homes and workplaces may be side-by-side, but the people in them are strangers. They neither touch nor share their feelings or thoughts about the "real stuff" of life. "We are," according to Dr. Allan Bloom, "social solitaries."[1] We have lost our sense of community.

Bloom goes on to say, "The most visible sign of our increasing separateness and, in its turn, the cause of ever greater separateness is divorce. . . . The important lesson the family taught was the existence of the only unbreakable bond, for better or worse, between human beings. . . . The decomposition of this bond is surely America's most urgent social problem."[2]

Husbands and wives who find themselves in conflict may have no other person with whom they can share the deep concerns of life before they reach crisis proportions. The demand for professional mental health providers is mute testimony that many people have to "hire" someone to be their friend. Most counselors readily admit they are filling a void for people who have no sense of a nurturing community. In our competitive pursuit for personal peace and prosperity, there is little room for simple, friendly relationships. Divorce is but a symptom of this problem of discontinuity among people, and it leads to an even greater breakdown of bonds that hold people together.

Our lack of community is most regrettable in the church, which should be a haven for lonely, alienated people. Many churches have a lot of activities but often fail to provide a sense of unity and oneness of spirit. They are preaching-teaching-learning centers, social activity centers, fund-raising centers. Members have a lot of associations—but few close friendships.

Most church groups tend to be task-oriented. The tendency, in such a ministry, is to avoid time-consuming people problems, and focus, instead, on structural or educational goals. But the story from the Gospels of the shepherd leaving the ninety-nine sheep to look for the one that was lost shows us that God's goals are not always man's goals. He calculates human worth on a different scale from ours. To him, the single lost sheep is more precious than the whole flock, which might be working diligently away inside the fold, not knowing—or caring—that one is still missing.

Because of this widespread lack of concern for individuals' needs, church leaders don't know what's happening in parishioners' homes and marriages. Many pastors are taken by surprise when couples in their churches separate and divorce. They are shocked, even outraged. But then the couple is often angry and resentful against the church or pastor who would assume to judge their personal life. They say, "Who does the pastor think he is to censor me or my actions? He doesn't even know me!"

The mere idea of such church discipline as discussed in a number of the Pauline Epistles seems foreign to the modern church member. It smacks of the hateful excesses of a loveless inquisition, rather than a caring act of reconciliation. The disciplined member doesn't view it as brothers and sisters rescuing a friend from spiritual disaster. The erring individual often has never felt love and concern in other ways from this community of believers.

We need a restoration of the distinctive mark of love for one another which characterized the first century church.[3] Lost is the cohesive power of breaking bread together and sharing fellowship around our common heritage in Jesus Christ. The privitization and isolation of our lives from other Christians, and the timidity of the church in attacking this heresy, is one of our most urgent problems. Whether we want to admit it or not, we have adopted the world's value of "live and let live." The other side of this is a smug indifference which says to the wounded and lonely church member, "Be self-reliant. Stand on your own two feet. Work out your own problems."

There is a tendency in the church not to deal with people's problems on an intimate level. "Couples who cannot 'get pregnant' do not come forward to be anointed, and neither does the impotent man nor the frigid woman. . . . Many affairs would never happen in the first place if the church could be the church on the intimate level where we all live."[4] I believe this attitude is largely to blame for the church's inability to intervene in marital conflicts. The result has been a steadily increasing divorce rate among Christians.

Because of our alienation and isolation, we are unable graciously and lovingly to restore those who are suffering the pain of divorce. Ed Dayton observes:

> The problem is that we, American Christians, have a secular mind. Many of us no longer think like Christians. Our lives have been so imbedded in our society that we think pretty much like everyone else in society. . . . The world is longing to believe that there are groups of men and women whose commitment to one another transcends materialism, competitiveness, and individualism. The cost of American values is more than we can bear. We have been robbed of a sacred gift: The ability to be committed to other human beings.[5]

This lack of communality is also seen in the very fabric of family relationships. Husbands, wives, and older children experience continual pressure to spin off in their own orbits. Family members often parallel each other, leading totally separate lives except when they intersect briefly to eat out of the same refrigerator and to sleep in the same house. Some Christian families sincerely desire a greater sense of cohesiveness against philosophical, economic, and social forces which would pull them apart. Sadly, the church that should support them in this goal can further fragment them with its numerous programs. Nightly programs for various age groups pull family members away from each other. Programs such as family evenings at home, with attendant curricular resources, would do more to build a spiritual and emotional bond among family members than a variety of diverse church-centered programs.

It is not enough to identify the loss of a real sense of community, and Christian community in particular. To do that is just to play an "ain't it awful?" game! If the church is going to minister healing in this matter of divorce, we must ask, "What kind of Christian community is equipped to deal with the relational concerns of God's people?"

The Christian community can help to heal relationship wounds through at least three necessary qualities: prophetic, supportive, and promise-making.

A PROPHETIC COMMUNITY

First, the church must be a prophetic community. It will model the balance between the tasks of reaching the lost and nurturing the people of God. Gary Collins describes this balanced life so clearly: "The Church is an evangelizing, preaching, teaching, discipling, sending community. It also must be a therapeutic community where people find love, acceptance, forgiveness, support, hope, encouragement, burden-bearing, caring, meaning, opportunities for service, challenge, and help in time of need."[6]

When the evangelistic task is overemphasized and the nurturing role is downplayed, the church risks spiritual burnout, especially among its overworked leaders. When outreach is underemphasized, however, the church can become a mental health center, forgetting its missionary calling. The church must find the balance to be, in Elizabeth O'Connor's words, on a "journey inward and a journey outward," (probably in that order).

For some couples, marital conflicts are petty and mostly just irritating. The message of the coming Kingdom, with its ethical

111

and spiritual claim on lives, may be the incentive needed to get out of an accusing, nagging rut. Such individuals will respond to a call to become involved in a crusade that is bigger than their pettiness. They recognize that when they are healed themselves, they can have a part in God's redemptive plan to restore mankind from human failure and sin.

For those couples who have divorced and remarried, the church has a responsibility not only to declare God's desire for people to keep their promises to one another, but to support them in ways to make that a reality. The church provides models for lifelong commitments, which are witnesses to God's grace and power in a world of broken promises. Those who have been alienated and now restored have a special empathy for the multitudes still outside the gates. The prophetic church gets such people involved in their outreach.

What we have come to know in Draconian terms as "church discipline" does not have to be cast in such an evil light. Promises have been broken; relationships have been severed; spirits have been wounded. Biblically based church discipline can be a method by which people can be loved back to health.

The church's function is to facilitate repentance, cleansing, renewal, and restoration. *A Guide to Church Discipline* by J. Carl Laney casts this intervention process in softer redemptive tones:

> Church discipline is not designed to punish but to restore. It is an act of healing. Yes, it may be painful; as in the application of iodine, pain is the price of a cleansed wound. It prepares the way for restoration. Through the pain of confrontation, rebuke, confession and forgiveness, the sinner is brought back into fellowship with Christ and His church. Such restoration is church discipline's ultimate goal.[7]

When it is church leaders who have sinned relationally, the church may be tempted to cover up or ignore the behavior, contrary to God's commands. Laney addresses this issue as well:

> True restoration doesn't mean we ignore the sin or pretend it is less serious than it is. It doesn't mean we exercise mercy

and neglect genuine guilt and accountability. But true restoration does mean we deal with a fallen leader in a Christlike manner—with compassion, forgiveness and genuine desire to assist in the healing process. It means we as church members and leaders come alongside the fallen warrior. To listen to his story, to encourage repentance, to offer assurance of forgiveness. To instruct from the Word. To pray for the rekindling of spiritual vitality.[8]

This kind of community not only retains its fidelity to Christian ethics and biblical teaching on church discipline, but it does so in a manner which allows for restoration and peace. Such caring confrontation is sound practice both theologically and psychologically. This kind of Christian community is much too scarce!

A SUPPORTIVE COMMUNITY

In addition to its prophetic function, the church must also be a supportive community. This calls for a depth of engagement with one another which goes beyond the superficial. It requires a level of progressive openness which allows us to see both the good and the bad in each other. It is a call for a new level of intimacy. We can't creatively minister to those we don't really know!

A number of years ago, my family had the opportunity to live communally in a Christian fellowship for two years. We were warned shortly after joining this fellowship that we would soon discover weaknesses within the membership. The more we got to know these people, the more we saw some areas where they still needed to grow—and they saw the same in us. Just as in a marriage, we saw them—and they saw us—"warts and all." Yet, no one was rejected for his or her idiosyncrasies. In the midst of human woundedness we saw the beauty of the work of the Lord in the lives of people committed to him.

We came away from that two-year experience permanently ruined on any kind of shallow fellowship which counterfeited the real intimacy and closeness found in that community of Christians. Hypocrisy flees in real community. We do not need to pretend to be what we are not; we are accepted as we are. We do not need the masks we may wear for protection out in an uncaring world; we can dare to be transparent. We do not need to carry our anxieties alone; here are friends who know how to bear one another's burdens. Finger pointing and "ain't it awful?" gossip have no place in such a community.

Instead, we are called to a new level of humility, where we acknowledge our own woundedness. In the words of Henri Nouwen, we become "wounded healers" of one another. We respond to the Lord's care by showing that care to others. As the apostle Paul writes: "Praise be to the God and Father of our Lord Jesus Christ, the Father of compassion and the God of all comfort, who comforts us in all our troubles so that we can comfort those in any trouble with the comfort we ourselves have received from God" (2 Cor. 1:4–5 NIV).

This is not the kind of fellowship for those who must appear to have it all together. But it is open to anyone who recognizes his or her own woundedness and unrighteousness apart from God's grace. People in such a Body become ministers to those in need, whatever their failures.

M. Scott Peck states in his book, *The Different Drum— Community Making and Peace:*

> Community is and must be inclusive. The great enemy of community is exclusivity. Groups that exclude others because they are poor or doubters or divorced or sinners or of some different race or nationality are not communities; they are cliques—actually defensive bastions against community . . . true communities . . . are always reaching to extend themselves. . . . Communities do not ask, "How can we justify taking this person in?" Instead the question is, "Is it at all justifiable to keep this person out?"[9]

The church needs to find ways to include singles in its family. Although many churches advertise ministries to the whole family, they have little to offer to unattached adults: young singles, single parents, divorced people, widows, and widowers. The church family is too often associated primarily with the nuclear family, and, thus, in a *de facto* way, becomes an exclusive club for the married. I am convinced that many young adults and divorced people are subtly pressured by loneliness into unwise and hasty marriages because the church has no ministry for them as singles.

We stopped by to see a good friend, a single parent with a four-year-old daughter about a year ago. Sharon's life had been difficult as she faced all the normal pressures of parenting alone. But her daughter was at least old enough now to talk and was providing some companionship. And, Sharon mentioned, she was part of a single adults group at her church. They happened to be going to a Milwaukee Brewers baseball game the next day. Six months later, she called to tell us she was engaged to a fellow she met that day on the way to the baseball game!

The creative church can find all kinds of opportunities for ministry to single adults—potlucks, hayrides, skating parties, progressive dinners, horseback riding, ice cream socials, tennis and golf tournaments. The list could go on and on. There can be a special effort to include singles (and their children) in holiday and birthday celebrations. When solo parenting becomes a struggle, a church family could adopt that family and do things with them. Deacons could become very creative in anticipating practical as well as personal needs of people living alone.

A church can really be a family that is just as close as our biological families. A number of years ago, my wife and three young sons remained in San Diego while I was on a six-month deployment to the Western Pacific as a navy chaplain. (Our extended families all live in the Midwest.) Our church there thought of many ways of ministering to my family: when our car got two flat tires just sitting in our driveway, someone came to repair them. When my wife was discouraged with parenting three pre-school boys, a father and son frequently picked them up to go to the beach or to play soccer. When neighbor kids threw a rock through a kitchen window, a fellow from the church came before dark to repair it so my wife would feel safe. On a holiday when other families were planning special outings, the pastor and his wife took my wife and boys to an amusement park and to a cookout at their house. When my wife needed to get out and be with other adults, the church offered a weekday morning Bible study and provided child care. And when she was really feeling alone on her birthday, a friend from the church came by to take her and our sons to the ice cream store she owned, to enjoy whatever treat they chose—not even knowing it was my wife's birthday! (But the Lord knew, and our friend knew the Lord!)

When individual churches are not large enough to have full-scale programs of their own, several local churches could band together to provide for the needs of singles. The church's message to single adults needs to be clear: You are a whole person in Christ! An unmarried individual is not incomplete and useless like half of a pair of scissors! We need, by both attitudes and actions, to create an environment in our churches that helps singles feel at home. When this happens, many unmarried or previously married people may begin to feel it's O.K. to be single; and when we share this attitude of acceptance, we may help them become a great ministry asset to the church.

A PROMISE-MAKING COMMUNITY

Finally, we need to be a promise-making community. We all make hasty choices and unwise decisions, and then go back on our word from time to time. Some people have a great fund of information and positive modeling in their formative years; others lack such an inheritance and struggle with even the most basic of human relations skills. Some have known a loving and forgiving God from infancy; others have decided that God is angry or indifferent as a result of their years of abuse or neglect. This impacts not just educational and vocational issues; it affects our relational skills and our faithfulness to our commitments.

Promise-keeping is not just between husband and wife. As a young father, I was very cautious when it came to making promises to my sons. If I made a promise, I tried very hard to keep it, even when I didn't feel like it (and it's sometimes hard to feel like playing football with a two-year-old son). As my sons grew older, they would put up an awful fuss if I tried to back out of this kind of commitment. They would whine, "But you promised, Dad!" And, usually, with such a reminder, I felt obligated to follow through on that promise.

Today my sons expect promises to be kept! Even though that does not always happen, they will carry that expectation into their adult relationships. Some children grow up in environments where promises are repeatedly broken. When those children become young adults, a commitment to God or to other human beings has a whole different connotation. It might be just an act of convenience to achieve a personal goal. More often than we'd like to think, marriage promises are made by individuals who are more eager to satisfy their own needs than their partner's. Such vows endure as long as the spouses love—rather than as long as they live!

C. S. Lewis expresses his own strong views on making marriage vows:

> Justice . . . includes the keeping of promises. Now everyone who has been married in a church has made a public, solemn promise to stick to his (or her) partner till death. . . . To this some may reply that he regarded the promise made in church as a mere formality and never intended to keep it. Whom then was he trying to deceive when he made it? God? That was really very unwise. Himself? That was not very much wiser. The bride, or bridegroom, or the in-laws? That was treacherous. Most often, I think, the couple (or one of them) hoped to deceive the public. They wanted the respectability that is attached to marriage without intending to pay the price: That is, they were imposters, they cheated. If they are still contented cheats, I have nothing to say to them: Who would urge the high and hard duty of chastity on people who have not wished to be merely honest? If they have now come to their senses and want to be honest, their promise, already made, constrains them. . . . If people do not believe in permanent marriage, it is perhaps better that they should live together unmarried than that they should make vows they do not mean to keep. It is true that by living together without marriage they will be guilty (in Christian eyes) of fornication. But one fault is not mended by adding another: Unchastity is not improved by adding perjury.[10]

Every day, couples approach the wedding altar with varying degrees of understanding and willingness to make and keep promises. Some husbands and wives can be absolutely nonchalant about their wedding vows. But the success of the marriage obviously depends upon this very thing. Craig Dykstra, professor of Christian Education at Princeton Theological Seminary, says: "Families are people who make promises to each other. When we see what those promises are, we see what a family is."[11]

He goes on to say that marriage is essentially promise-making and promise-keeping: "How do people get married? How does a person become a husband or a wife? It is by making a promise, by saying, 'I promise . . .' or 'I take thee . . .' or 'I will . . .' or 'I do'! That is it. An act of promising constitutes a marriage. It, in and of itself, creates a family. To be a spouse, to be a wife or husband in relation to someone else, means nothing else but to have made some promises."[12]

We do sometimes fail to keep our promises, but whether such failure is fatal depends on the frequency and circumstances of broken promises:

> It is promise-making, not promise-keeping, that constitutes the family. . . . We fail for all sorts of reasons. We may fail because of certain cultural, social, and economic forces beyond our control . . . or we may fail because of our human limitations . . . or we may fail because of our own sinfulness . . . It is not the failure to keep promises, in and of itself, that destroys family. Such failure happens in every family and can be expected. Family can remain family in the midst of unfulfilled promises. What destroys family is the collapse of promise-making. It is when the very making of promises is no longer believed and believed in that families die. The failure to keep promises and the collapse of promise-making are, of course, related. The continual failure to fulfill promises acts as a corrosive to the promise-making, so that there may come a time when the lack of fulfillment destroys the very meaning and significance of promise-making. But when this happens, it is the promise-making itself that becomes null and void. Then the constituting ground of family is dissolved. In divorce, for example, a certain set of promises are no longer being made. The promise-making that constitutes two persons as

husband and wife comes to an end. That is what makes them no longer husband and wife.[13]

Pastors and Christian counselors are in the business of helping people keep their faith promises to one another and to the Lord himself. Psychologists say congruence is an essential component of healthy human relationships. Theologians speak of faithfulness and perseverance as marks of spiritual maturity. Ethicists call credibility and honesty characteristics of the good citizen.

In other words, all of these professionals are conscious of the implications of individual action, both as a way to maintain personal integrity but also influencing society at large. Pastors are stewards both to the individual as well as to the fellowship of believers, calling our people to have faith and be faithful. This is just another way in which the Christian world view conflicts with humanism's emphasis on individualism and privatization of our lives.

Sheldon Vanauken, in "The (False) Sanction of Eros" from *Under the Mercy,* looks at marriage partners who fail to keep their vows. He further addresses the fact that divorce is not a "victimless crime":

> We all know that countless marriages are wrecked by one of the spouses falling in love with what used to be called the 'Other Woman' or her male counterpart. And, since art follows life, the modern novels and films are full of triangles and betrayals. But let us notice how often the storyteller sets it up so that the betrayed spouse more or less deserves it as being unkind, unloving, or a bit of a bore. Scarlet letters are no longer in fashion. Our sympathies are with the lovers, not with the betrayed spouse. . . . And never—never once in any novel or film I can think of—does the betraying spouse seriously think of the meaning of broken promises. Both duty and the given word are, like honour, merely wretched remnants of the 'middle ages.' The Spirit of the Age proclaims sexual love to be the greatest good. In the books and films we share the happiness of the happy lovers: love itself is lovable. The lovers may experience difficulties—uncooperative spouses and superiors— so that we may share their anguish; but the lovers must

never face up to the real meaning of betrayal of their vows, for that would mar their happy love. . . . The Spirit of the Age—not the Holy Spirit—ceaselessly proclaims erotic love (or even barnyard sex) to be the ultimate good; and therefore anything that stands in its way, solemn vows, duty, loyalty, the words of Our Lord, is seen as chains upon the soaring human spirit.[14]

Since the family of God is made up of a cluster of individual families, it is only as strong as its weakest link. If a church is largely filled with highly neurotic or immature Christians, that church will be characterized by such behavior. If the church is mostly made up of people who have a very sloppy understanding of commitment, those people will have neglectful relationships with marriage partners and a shallow engagement with other church members.

Every family in the church needs to realize that their relationships in the home and within the Body of Christ are not a private matter. Craig Dykstra, writing about family promises, says:

Family promising is no longer merely private. Family promising is no longer something between two or a few persons (the kinship family alone). When family promises are incorporated into our discipleship promises and the family itself is incorporated into the family of the household of God, our family promises and activities become the concern of the whole church. This means the end of any attitude that suggests "What I and my family do is our business and nobody else's." As Christians together, even though we are not kin, the character and quality of "my" family promise-making is your business, too, just as these matters in "your" life are "my" business. We have a responsibility now for each other's family promises—the making and breaking of them, the fulfilling and non-fulfilling of them. It is a responsibility that requires of us not only mutual concern, care, and support but also mutual instruction and even discipline in these matters. We have now both the freedom and the responsibility to be involved in each other's family life.[15]

From a Christian perspective, we do have a responsibility for one another. We are called to intimacy and involvement in others' lives on an everyday basis. Then when the storms hit, we have that history of faithful friendship, and we receive permission to intervene in others' lives.

PASTORAL INTERVENTION

Even within the church family where a sense of oneness and communality exists, the pastor has the primary responsibility—and opportunity—to intervene in marital/divorce problems. Ideally, much of this intervention will be of the preventive type.

There are both informal and formal approaches that intervention may take. Informally, pastors can make their people sensitive to the typical pressures on their marriages. Practical, yet biblical, teaching related to grace and forgiveness, guilt and anger, and conflict and communication are just a few topics to be built into preaching and teaching. Modern-day issues of existentialism, individualism, materialism, and competitiveness can be brought under the light of Scripture in Christian education classes.

Premarital counseling must not only be mandatory, but imply serious consideration by the Body of Christ on the wisdom of marriage by the couple. Nothing should be assumed! Jason Towner writes, "When church boards and congregations become concerned about the (wedding) ceremonies they permit to be performed, divorce rates will go down. When we make engagements, weddings, and marriages matters of intense prayer by the community of faith, divorce rates will go down. When the body of believers stands by to undergird and support newly created homes, divorce rates will go down."[16]

Cellular fellowship groups, with undershepherds appointed and trained by a pastor/counselor team, will accomplish much of the relationship building. Within the small group, intimacy develops to care for the concerns of God's people. When significant problems are identified, pastoral care and counseling resources can be quickly alerted. Couples contemplating divorce or those who are struggling with the after-effects of divorce will both profit from this individual attention and care. In summary, informal approaches can teach people how to live as Christians in a non-Christian world and provide a friendship/fellowship network to monitor and support that process.

Formal interventions are designed, on the other hand, for those not interested in cell groups or those with more complex problems than peer counselors can manage. Very early in my pastoral ministry, I was confronted with a problem that was beyond my capabilities. A young Christian wife and mother of two pre-schoolers was the subject of repeated beatings by an alcoholic husband. From information I could gather, the children also suffered at his hand. They all appeared on my doorstep late one night with fear in their eyes. They were scared to go home and yet scared to take steps to have the husband arrested. The immediate need was to find safe shelter for her and the children. Then, over the next weeks, frequent home visits, counseling, and conversations with community mental health professionals helped insure some degree of safety and sanity for this family. It is important for the pastor to know when to call for help.

Crisis counseling or rehabilitative counseling for habituated problems calls for one of several levels of professional expertise.

At the first level, it involves a vigorous home-visitation program by a mature, trained eldership. These elders should have a willingness to participate in this sometimes traumatic, and always time-consuming ministry. Such visitation communicates concern and provides the pastoral staff with information regarding troublesome situations within the fellowship. In some churches elders have opened their homes to newcomers rather than using the home-visitation approach.

At the second level, a formal intervention program includes communication skills improvement and Marriage Enrichment/ Encounter. We somehow assume couples know how to really listen to each other. That may not be true.

This level of intervention may include formal pastoral counseling for conflicts in marriage. Pastors attempting interventions will find a complex variety of problems that they may feel unable to handle. But most pastors can offer significant counsel, particularly if they have a working relationship with a Christian psychologist to whom they can refer counselees with significantly complex crises beyond their level of expertise.

The third level involves professional therapy by family systems counselors. Divorce, divorce recovery, and remarriage are all traumatic events. Some people cumulatively feel the pain of divorce until it becomes completely incapacitating, especially at holidays. Jason Towner describes a friend trying to face Christmas as a divorced father:

> My friend had tried to solo Christmas and had almost succeeded in convincing everyone around the Christmas tree that he was not hurting. He laughed; he played with his two kids; he ate the goodies—but inside he bled. When the moment came that he had to return his children to their mother and go home alone to face his bed on Christmas Eve night, he could not. He checked himself into the hospital. My phone rang early Christmas morning.
>
> I had never been in a mental hospital before. I got there during the middle of visiting hours. We began talking about this and that. I took off all my psychological clothes so that I could talk with him. He wasn't crazy or mentally ill—he just could not cope with being so hurt.[17]

Such a reaction is not all that uncommon. It can be an emotional reaction or a physical reaction, or both. It can come months after the divorce itself, especially if divorced people haven't been given the opportunity to openly grieve over their loss. People just find themselves incapable of coping with the pain of rejection, failure, and limitations brought on by the separation. They need pastoral or clinical help—or both—to sort things out.

As the pastor and counselor work closely together, clients continue to receive the love and support of the church while working through some very difficult psychological and ethical dilemmas. The sensitive counselor will recognize the spiritual renewal that needs to take place, and will welcome the pastor's insight. Along with an enabling and redemptive body of Christians, a pastor/counselor team can contribute to the health and effectiveness of the church.

It takes effort to create a real sense of community within the Christian church. This involves both formal and informal programs that build bridges to our people so that we become aware of needs and are prepared to respond caringly to them.

Even believers fail. We can respond to them as we would to fallen warriors, offering forgiveness and restoration to those who seek new beginnings. We can recognize their woundedness and offer our unconditional love and support. We're there to help them learn to make new promises, and we model the committed lifestyle ourselves.

As Christians, we must ask forgiveness for our own individualistic, island-like approach to living. The Lord expects more openness and vulnerability from his people. "Carry each other's burdens, and in this way you fulfill the law of Christ" (Gal. 6:2 NIV). We rejoice in our dependence upon our brothers and sisters. We cannot say we love God with all our hearts and exclude our neighbor from our lives. The apostle John writes, "If anyone says, 'I love God,' yet hates his brother, he is a liar. For anyone who does not love his brother, whom he has seen, cannot love God whom he has not seen. And He has given us this command: Whoever loves God must also love his brother" (1 John 4:20–21).

The Christian community is faced with a great challenge: "Divorce presents an opportunity for the family of God, enabled by the indwelling of the Spirit of Christ, to demonstrate to a hostile world its greatest attribute—concern for one another. In this moment of testing, the church is at its best—portraying God's kind of love—unmerited, but unlimited."[18]

CHAPTER EIGHT

THE CHALLENGE OF REMARRIAGE

ADAPTING TO NEW RELATIONSHIPS

Sometimes we'd all like a second chance. It might have been after failing a test in school or striking out in softball. Down deep in our hearts, we have said, "Gimme a break. Let me try just one more time. I know I can do it!"

This doesn't change when we grow older. We still have a desire to try to recoup our losses, learn by our mistakes, and try again. We'll try harder next time. We'll do it smarter.

This is the attitude of many who have made marital mistakes. With divorce comes an enormous sense of failure. Some divorced people feel thoroughly defeated by divorce, but most want to try marriage again.

Several years ago, my sons and I curled up on our sofa, armed with sodas and a bag of chips to watch a television program about a National Football League team entitled "Second Season." That team had a lot of talent, but in the first part of the season, they made error after error and they lost one game after another.

Sometime around midseason, television cameras followed the team as they went through a Monday afternoon autopsy of their most recent defeat. The coach pointed out a number of factors which contributed to their loss: missed blocks, dropped balls, sloppy tackles, and mistimed plays. All of these mistakes were acutely obvious to players watching the postgame films.

But rather than just stop there, the coach pinpointed areas where individual players could improve technique and eliminate bad habits. The next week in practice the team concentrated on those specifics. Linemen who were repeatedly off-sides had to go through drills to concentrate to control that reflex. Receivers had to practice holding on to the ball. Linebackers went through drills to make effective tackles. Running backs practiced sprinting through holes. As the saga unfolded, the combination of practice, teamwork, and motivation paid off. The team learned from mistakes. They were victorious in all the rest of the games in their "second season."

Divorced people want to find pastors and counselors who will coach them in their "second season." Pastors may first see such couples when the man and woman are looking for someone to officiate at their wedding. Counselors meet such couples in their divorce-recovery workshops or single-parent support groups. Sometimes pastors and counselors don't encounter remarried couples until they need crisis counseling, months or years after the wedding. The attitudes with which these helping professionals and their clients approach the remarriage may determine to a large degree how successful the "second season" will be.

CLERGY ATTITUDES TOWARD REMARRIAGE

The pastor's attitude toward remarriage opens or closes the door of the church to divorced couples wanting to remarry. If the client hears that remarriage following divorce is the "unpardonable sin," which, once committed, forever seals one's spiritual fate, then there is little value in practicing one's faith.

Where divorce is viewed as sin, but forgivable sin, then a renewed life of service and fellowship can be experienced.

For most pastors and Christian counselors, there is little problem with remarriage for those who have been abandoned by former spouses. Nor is there a conflict in blessing a remarriage if the former marriage was broken by adultery. If one of the partners has an ex-spouse who has remarried, then the original marriage bond is severed and many pastors would explore remarriage with the couple. I would personally want to hear the words and see the fruits of a repentant heart in such a case.

Some pastors accept already remarried people into the church and into certain levels of service and ministry if there is evidence of genuine repentance for sin and an openness to receive instruction and counsel prior to application for membership.

The real problem for pastors arises in being asked to officiate at the second wedding for partners when at least one of these partners has an unremarried spouse who is willing to reconcile. It is ethically and biblically impossible to sanction such a marriage. The Christian approach in this case must be to discourage remarriage and encourage reconciliation efforts.

This would also hold true for Christians who have been divorced on other than biblical grounds from former spouses who have not remarried. Most pastors would want to exhaust every avenue for individuals to be reconciled to prior mates.

Christians are called to a high level of kingdom ethics and are enabled by God's grace to live uprightly. This may involve pastoral counsel to live as single persons seeking reconciliation, rather than compound the sin of covenant-breaking by a remarriage. Many pastors feel remarriage irrevocably closes the door to return to one's spouse. (See Matt. 19:9, 12.) This is neither popular counsel to give nor to receive. Our society would tell us that individuals have a right to self-fulfillment and personal happiness. However, Charles Swindoll, in his book *Strike the Original Match*, argues for an opposite point of view:

Our ultimate goal, our highest calling in life is to glorify God—not to be happy. Let that sink in! Glorifying Him is our greatest pursuit. Not to get our way. Not to be comfortable. Not to find fulfillment. Not even to be loved or to be appreciated or to be taken care of. Now these are important, but they are not primary. As I glorify Him, He sees to it that other essential needs are met. . . . or my need for them diminishes.[1]

It is understandable, then, that pastors have an aversion to officiating at remarriage ceremonies. If they could, most pastors would simply avoid the complex problems associated with placing God's blessing upon marriages following divorce. But that's not possible, short of counseling divorced people to marry outside of the church and go through this transition with little support from the church or clergy.

CLIENT ATTITUDES TOWARD REMARRIAGE

Because of the ethical problems the church has with divorce, many remarried couples avoid Christian fellowships for fear of judgment. They know the promarriage stance of the church and its expectation that Christians remain faithful to their spouses. Divorced persons come to a "black hole" in their spiritual walk. For many, their relationship with God and his people terminated with their decision to divorce and remarry. That doesn't mean they don't have a spiritual hunger, however. They just recognize that some pastors will find it hard to minister to them at this particular change-point in their lives. So, they tend to keep the church at arm's length until a major crisis emerges in their lives that forces them to get help.

When divorced individuals begin to consider remarriage, they struggle with a variety of feelings. They have already experienced one failure in marriage, but they want a second chance. Abigail Trafford, writing in *Crazy Time: Surviving Divorce*, states:

For most people, being divorced is a transition period between marriages. Statistics show that five out of six divorced men and three out of four divorced women eventually remarry. Most remarriages take place within three years of the divorce date. In the California Children of Divorce

Project Study 43 percent of the men and 33 percent of the women remarried within five years of the separation date. The dark side of remarriage is redivorce. . . . The depressing statistical fact is that the redivorce rate for people who have been married and divorced before is double the divorce rate for people in a first marriage.[2]

Someone once joked that remarriage is "the triumph of hope over experience." Many couples do not learn enough about themselves and their negative traits during their first marriage and divorce. That increases the probability they will make the same mistakes with someone new. Plus, that new person brings his or her own emotional baggage to the relationship. Strangely enough, that new spouse can turn out to be very much like the previous spouse, both positively and negatively. As Robert Kirsch, a family therapist, observes: "One way to stay married even though you divorce your spouse is to repeat the relationship over and over again."[3]

We know "hope springs eternal. . . ." But is this enough of a reason to take a chance on remarriage? Most people have at least some positive memories of their marriage, and they miss those good times. Probably a majority of divorced persons see more faults in their ex-spouses than in themselves. The conclusion, then, is simply, "I made a bad choice. I'll be a more discriminating shopper this time. I'll find someone who will suit my needs better."

The problem is divorced people do not want a "repeat performance" of their last marriage. As Jason Towner points out,

> "Re" involves repetition. If it is to be healthy, a marriage must stand on its own merits, never in comparison to or in contrast with another marriage. But some people discover they have gone "from the frying pan into the fire." Some are so glad that their new love does not have their first love's faults that they overlook the faults they do possess.[4]

This can be a prescription for future disillusionment.

Divorce always carries with it a sense of failure. Often there are troublesome wounds from the past that have to heal before

129

one can make good decisions. The choice of a new mate is premature until the whole rationale for remarriage is evaluated.

"Mel Krantzler speaks of persons who marry to fill 'the poisonous needs' that they felt in the first two years after their divorces: What are the poisonous needs?

—I can't manage these kids by myself.
—I can't support myself.
—I need someone to take care of me.
—I just want some good home cooking again.
—I'll show her (him) that I can get along without her (him) and that others want me.
—I'm afraid to be alone."[5]

The danger in such motivations is that they are all dependency orientated, aimed at finding a rescuer. These needs can so overpower a person that he or she becomes desperate rather than discriminating in the search for a mate. Such desperation can lead to a disastrous choice of a new life partner.

A forty- or fifty-year-old divorced person, man or woman, can resemble a seventeen-year-old who is intoxicated with the pleasurable new relationship. That individual, feeling young and free again, plunges headfirst into a second marriage. Yes, "the grass is always greener on the other side of the fence," but, as James Dobson quips, "it still has to be mowed."[6]

The path toward remarriage can be a positive affirmation of life and an end to the period of mourning. Remarriage also marks a significant act of reembracing life and the willingness to risk. Thus it generates two attitudes that are quite different: a counselor's attitude of concern and questions about motives, and the couple's attitude of hope and determination.

READINESS FOR REMARRIAGE

How can a pastor or counselor know that these two divorced people are ready for remarriage? How can the couple themselves know? What are key factors to look for? Both the couple and the counselor will want to recognize what went wrong in the past relationship(s). Do those factors exist in the present situation? Has the divorced person(s) been able to deal with the woundedness from his or her past relationship? Are they both free of habituated problems from their troubled past—alcohol/drug abuse, workaholic patterns, flirtatious behavior, spouse abuse, family violence, sexual dysfunction? Have they learned to express deep feelings and troublesome thoughts? Do they know how to "fight fair"? Do they share similar values and goals? Are they willing and mature enough to accept stepparenting responsibilities?

Couples who honestly face all of these issues and sort them out greatly enhance their chances of success in a second marriage. But the reality is that pastors and counselors often don't see a couple until after the remarriage—and after problems in many of these areas have multiplied. Divorced people wanting to remarry often have short courtships. Besides, these couples suspect ministers will disapprove of their remarriage, so they tend to avoid premarital counsel. Issues that could have been interdicted in the premarital stage now beg for attention.

Pastors then may have a kind of "I-told-you-so" attitude. Persons may even get a lecture much like the one a dentist gives to cavity-prone patients who have failed to floss and brush faithfully. That may not do much good. When the "patient" recognizes the need, he or she will comply with the professional's wishes—and not before.

I'm reminded of the story in the popular film, *The Natural.* It tells of a young baseball player with great promise who, due to his own foolishness, was shot and wounded by a girlfriend. That terminated a budding pitching career. Later on in life, the main character makes a comeback as a centerfielder and slugger in the major leagues. Suddenly his old injury ruptures, and he is hospitalized with little hope of playing baseball ever again. A childhood sweetheart stops by to see him and he laments, "Some mistakes I guess we never stop paying for."

She responds by saying, "I believe we have two lives: The life we learn with and the life we live after that."

For couples starting over, there is this haunting feeling that one may continue to pay for past mistakes. Yet, concurrent with this feeling is a sense of wanting to learn by past experiences and do it right the second time around.

ADAPTING TO A NEW SPOUSE

Divorced people who have successful second marriages have acquired the flexibility to adapt to change and the perseverance to work through conflict. They understand early that adjustments will take time, patience, and hard work.

History plays a significant role in the success of a new marriage. For years, brides have been told to bring "something old" and "something new" to their weddings. All brides and bridegrooms bring with them childhood images and experiences of gender roles and communication patterns. Some also add years of abusive treatment as a result of family violence or drug and alcohol abuse. Previously married partners bring to the new relationship old issues from their previous marriage, including all the anger, resentments, and hurts.

Individuals bring new issues to the marriage, as well. They have expectations of great success or sometimes fear of failure. They bring caricatures of a faultless fiancée who will be able to satisfy their every longing. Previously married people often bring children to this new marriage. Sometimes these children will be expected to become instant friends of their new brothers and sisters, the children of the other partner.

What is brought to the new marriage can be quite formidable, even to the optimistic bride or bridegroom. As a counselor once told me, "Remarriage is a 'mixed bag' full of surprises. It's sort of like Halloween: You don't know until you get home and open up your bag under the porchlight whether you have tricks or treats." If the pastor or counselor can do premarital counseling, some of the nasty surprises can be identified before they become troublesome. The couple, with the counselor's help, can set realistic goals for their marriage and prevent some future conflicts.

But even when counselors don't see a couple until problems are already magnified, they can help clients sort out their histories. People bring into their relationships differing levels of maturity, intelligence, and social development. Consequently, some people learn quickly by listening to instructions and watching models. Some individuals learn only by trial and error. Emotionally immature individuals are almost doomed to repeat their mistakes.

Pastors also are interested in the spiritual maturity and integrity of the couple which will affect their adjustment to remarriage. Spouses who are fully committed to the Lord are far more likely to be selfless and committed to a new spouse. The Bible very plainly warns couples not to be "unequally yoked together" with unbelievers. If either person is living out of fellowship with God or unrepentant for past sinfulness, pastors cannot support plans for remarriage. Where the marriage has already taken place, the Christian partner can be encouraged to be a witness for Christ in the marriage.

Many who go through a divorce have a deep sense of spiritual failure. As a result, there can be a real spiritual "bottoming out" following divorce. If not resolved, these issues will threaten the new relationship before it has a chance to develop. The best counsel to offer a divorced person who has gone through a real spiritual crisis, and now is contemplating remarriage, is "Wait." Spiritual health and wholeness will return, but it will take time.

Recovery from divorce is more difficult for someone with a weak spiritual foundation prior to the divorce. Many immature believers have a poor image of God, major gaps in biblical knowledge and ethics, or negative experiences within the church which have retarded their spiritual development. Inner resources to cope with any difficulties are limited.

Such individuals perceive themselves as the victims of divorce. They are angry at a God who would allow divorce to ruin their lives. The fear and anger associated with a perceived abandonment by God must be dealt with to allow for spiritual rebirth.

Pastors and Christian counselors need to recognize issues of human responsibility and sin as primary causes of marital dissolution. This sinful behavior must be reckoned with and God's grace appropriated. At the same time, pastors and counselors see secondary contributing factors to divorce: impoverished environment, maladjusted personality, immature emotional-spiritual development, and poor communication skills. Spiritual, as well as emotional compatibility must be a priority in any new marriage for the Christian.

ADAPTING TO A NEW FAMILY

Couples who remarry following divorce not only have to adjust to each other, but often to their roles as parents to children who are virtual strangers. This instant family, referred to as a stepfamily or blended family, is often underestimated as a source of conflict in the new marriage. Actress Marlo Thomas, in marrying television talk-show host Phil Donahue eleven years ago, instantly became a stepmother to four boys and one girl. The four sons lived with their father. Thomas recounts her naive expectations regarding the marriage (her first):

> I went into this totally foolhardy. . . . I thought that I was marrying a man that I love and, by the way, he had these kids. For some reason my wisdom failed me. They were these little boys and they seemed so cool. I really wasn't seeing them as little children who needed a lot of attention. . . . I just hadn't been around children. . . . I wasn't ready for it at all. I went into it with my eyes closed a bit.[7]

Thomas's experience is common. Most remarried couples are unprepared for the complex and powerful net of relationships that make up a stepfamily. Furthermore, her experience is not isolated. The number of stepparents and stepchildren is growing. "At the present time one-half million adults become stepparents each year in the United States (and) one out of every six American children under eighteen is a stepchild."[8] Statistics also tell us "an estimated 4.5 million children live with their mother and a stepfather. . . . An additional 1 million live with a father and stepmother."[9]

Betty Carter, a social worker who is director of the Family Institute of Westchester County in Mount Vernon, New York, describes the dynamics of the change for a family upon remarriage: "The family starts along a two-lane road, but then takes a detour called divorce, single-parenting and then remarriage for some. They're now not on a two-lane road but on a six-lane super highway. The family members continue along in a much more complex form."[10] Strangers suddenly find themselves living together (often without their input) because two people decided to get married. The complexity of these relationships can easily be seen by using a wire diagram of the family tree (called a genogram). This is an excellent tool for pastors and counselors to use to gain an understanding of blended families as demonstrated in the diagram on page 136.

Certain predictable emotional issues emerge in remarriage. Each reconstituted family carries emotional baggage from three pasts: "From the family of origin, from the first marriage, (and) from the process of separation, divorce, and the period between marriages."[11] So, in a significant way, the ghosts from the past haunt stepfamilies. One by one, everyday events trigger emotional landmines. Meanwhile, stepparents are busy trying to cope with a confusing present and an uncertain future, as well.

Relationships within the new family are very ambiguous. There are few role models found in the nuclear family to guide in the strange land of blended families. Couples will encounter greater difficulty if they expect life to be predictable and well defined. It is more realistic for a couple to expect that things will be in flux for a while, with one crisis being dealt with at a time.

Before too long, it is hoped, family members will agree (at least in part) on the answers to certain boundary questions:

1) Membership (Who are the "real" members of the family?)
2) Space (What space is mine? Where do I really belong?)
3) Authority (Who is really in charge—of discipline? Money? Decisions?)
4) Time (Who gets how much of my time and how much do I get of theirs?)[12]

Counselors will also be concerned that sexual (incest) boundaries are established among children of blended families as well as between stepparents and stepchildren. As more and more children and adolescents live in families with no blood relationships and poor bonding, the danger of incidents of

THE JOHNSON FAMILY Presenting Problem: Conflict resulting from ex-spouse's interference in primary family and conflict between his (Fred's) children, her (Mary's) children and their child (Fred & Mary's daughter, Jennifer).

PRIMARY FAMILY

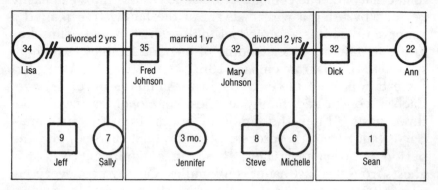

Symbols:

⚋	Divorce
(7)	7 yr. old female
[8]	8 yr. old male

Notes:

1. Lisa (Fred's ex-wife) resists Fred's efforts to have his children visit him in spite of a court order to do so. Fred retaliates by sporadic/late child-support payments. Fred's children don't like his new wife, Mary, and do not like her children (Steve & Michelle) nor their half sister (Jennifer). Visits to the Johnson home by Jeff and Sally often end in conflict.

2. Fred and Mary's relationship is good. They enjoy each other's company and are delighted with their new baby (Jennifer). Fred has a hard time bonding with Mary's children (Steve & Michelle) partially because Dick (Mary's ex-husband) constantly criticizes Fred in front of Steve & Michelle.

3. Dick's wife Ann is jealous of the amount of time he wants to spend with Steve & Michelle, rather than with their new baby Sean.

GENOGRAM OF KEY TRIANGLES IN REMARRIED FAMILIES

increases. Even in a Christian home, adolescent stepchildren can be encouraged to develop healthy brother-sister relationships.

Counselors can be genuinely helpful when they assure families that it's normal to confront certain issues in this blending process: Spouses' guilt over past marital behavior, children having loyalty conflicts, spouses trying too hard and expecting change too fast, and everyone avoiding conflict as a means of coping with fear of further hurt and separation. The financial situation is another problem area: Counselors continually are confronted with money problems between ex-spouses. Spouse or child support is often withheld by one partner in reprisal for limited visitation rights or dating behavior of the ex-spouse. Sometimes the financial situation is compounded by unemployment or the increased financial responsibility for a new family, and is the basis for a lot of resentment of spouses in a new marriage.

Life-cycle issues also play a significant role in the adjustment of spouses. Authors Monica McGoldrick and Elizabeth Carter state:

> In general, the wider the discrepancy in family life cycle experiences between the new spouses, the greater the difficulty of transition and the longer it will take to integrate a workable new family. . . . When the remarried spouses come together at the same phase of the family life cycle, they have the advantage of bringing the same life cycle tasks and the same general previous experience to the new family.[13]

All of these adjustments don't happen overnight. It takes time and patience to establish a new family. "The passage from newly married stepfamily to well-functioning stepfamily takes time— by most accounts a minimum of four years and sometimes as long as nine years. To be successful, the stepfamily must move through stages from a biologically-based mini-family to a unit with a strong, cooperative couple at the helm."[14]

Patricia Papernow, a psychiatrist in Newtonville, Massachusetts, identifies three stages of stepfamily adjustment:

The fantasy phase ("I'm so glad to have a new mother-father for my kids" or "I love my new partner, so, of course, I will love his-her kids"), the immersion phase ("Something is wrong here and it's my fault" or "Something's wrong here and I don't like it"), and the mobilization phase (where the step-parent rocks the boat rather than jumping ship or where both partners see themselves on the same side, trying to figure out how to resolve a complex set of family needs and problems).[15]

A CHRISTIAN RESPONSE

Stepfamilies have been with us for a long time. Often they have been overlooked by the church when it talks about and plans for "families." Usually the imagery is of television families like "The Waltons" or the Andersons of "Father Knows Best." The nuclear family is only one of several configurations of households in this day of divorce, single parenting, unwed couples living together, and remarriage.

Because the church has valued the concept of the nuclear family, it has perhaps been slow to design religious education materials or programs with single parents or blended families specifically in mind. Very few ministry efforts have been made to reach out to this growing population. What can the church realistically do for them?

Pastors and other helping professionals can assist stepfamilies in making the adjustment. They can help couples to understand their past and then help them come to terms with it. Children can be encouraged to admit their feelings of divided loyalties. Plans can be developed to tackle confrontations and keep them from getting ugly. Children can be reminded that it's normal and acceptable not to instantly love a stranger who happens to have married their mom or dad.

Of course, all of these recommendations assume that pastors, youth directors, and Christian education teachers are themselves aware of the issues of stepparent living. Once they are, they can more effectively minister to this growing number of needy families.

Stepfamilies often have a resource problem. They need support from counselors, pastors, schoolteachers, and other community helpers to assist them in the blending process. Family members frequently need someone outside the family to talk to (often on a peer level). These "outsiders" can give them some impartial feedback regarding the numerous conflicts going on in their lives. Here is a place where concerned Christian laypersons can be of immeasurable help in just being listening friends who provide a quiet lagoon of safety and sanity off from the raging river of change.

We can suggest several changes in our work with stepfamilies: 1) an acknowledgement that stepfamilies exist as a valid group for ministry, 2) the design of programs and literature specifically related to their needs, 3) an understanding by pastor and people of the issues which confront these reconstituted families, 4) intervention in families struggling with stepfamily relationships, and 5) selection of Christian laypersons who are stepparents and the enlisting of their help in forming a couples' support group for those starting blended families. A special concern is to establish good stepfamily models.

CONCLUSION

Starting over is hard for all of us, but particularly so for those who are divorced. Yet, it is possible to begin again! It will take a special kind of coaching from pastors or other counselors, and a unique form of courage from clients to have a successful "second season." It will call for large doses of repentance, faith, patience, and perseverance to establish a new marriage. It will involve climbing mountains of fear and doubt as well as walking through deep valleys of grief and despair. Yet, in between those extremes will be some breathtaking new perspectives of oneself and others that will enrich and challenge the divorced person courageous enough to try. Those who are dependent on the Lord for grace, strength, and guidance magnify their probability of success.

CHAPTER NINE

DIVORCE AND THE SEASONS OF LIFE

NOTHING IS LEFT UNQUESTIONED,
INCLUDING THE MARRIAGE

The changing of the seasons crept up on me almost impercepti-
bly. Physically, I began to notice a graying of my hair at the
edges. When I would play football with my boys, I noticed I
was not as quick as I used to be in my reactions. Gone forever
were the days of high-school football glory. I avoided mirrors
and scales as I begrudgingly headed to the clothing store for
trousers one size larger. My desire to turn back my body clock
was tantamount to attempting to prevent the autumn leaves
from turning color.

Psychologically, I was becoming bored and irritable at work,
mildly depressed over some of the choices I had made in my
life, and restless for a change that would offer me roots and
deeper relationships with others.

Spiritually, I had a growing awareness that my life on earth was half over, and I sensed a need for new beginnings. Theologically, I was becoming uncomfortable with some of the dogmatism of earlier years. Down deep, I felt a growing momentum for change within my spirit. The seasons were changing for me!

The first change for me was vocational. After a series of events, it became apparent to me that I should divest myself emotionally from the navy and move toward a teaching/counseling ministry in the civilian world. I experienced many mixed feelings as I grieved over leaving a way of life I had come to know and enjoy in some respects. Yet there was, in the midst of this transition, a real sense of adventure and risk which "stirred the juices" of creativity within my spirit. Like a trapeze artist building momentum with each pendulum-like swing high over the floor of the "big top," I knew very soon I would have to risk everything in letting go of the past to grasp a new way of life. I realized right then and there, adventure and security were antonyms.

In my self-absorption, I had failed to notice some of the seasonal changes that were occurring in my wife as well. Our school-age children were becoming less dependent upon her as her interests grew in a teaching/counseling ministry. I found myself with someone who had dreams of her own, as nature reminded her of her mortality. Issues of further education, career development, a need for "roots," and a concern for spiritual renewal pushed their way into our world. We discovered we were in the midst of a midlife crisis. This change of seasons would test our love for each other and force us to take risks we had not dared before. We have since discovered our situation is not that unusual for couples passing into their forties. Many couples our age were experiencing role conflict: vocational/relational dissatisfaction, and spiritual/existential questions which tested their marriages and, in some cases, led to divorce.

It is helpful for counselors to have an appreciation for stages of psychosocial development as we attempt to care for couples in crisis, particularly in the divorce-prone years of midlife. In this chapter I would like to look at the symptoms of developmental changes in adults, and the adjustments that must be made in order to live a productive and satisfying life. Throughout this process, I intend to focus on the tensions these changes create in marriages, specifically in the high threat era of middle age. A divorce-prevention counseling strategy will be outlined that will assist counselors as they intervene in the lives of couples in midlife transition.

THE REALITY OF CHANGING SEASONS

I grew up in the upper Midwest and was used to the changing seasons. I looked forward to the chirping sound of the first robin announcing spring, the droning of an outboard motor pushing a fishing boat across a lake telling me summer had come, and the roar of the crowd and beat of a band in a stadium as footballs filled the air declaring "Fall is here." Winter, however, was never a season I *liked* to see arrive. Though I *liked* the beauty of the first snowfall, winter represented hazardous driving, cars that wouldn't start, and staying indoors sheltered from the cold. Winter could stay away for all I cared.

The Issue of Timing

Whether we like it or not, life also is made up of seasons and transitions. If we synchronize ourselves with these rhythms, life can be enjoyable. However, if we fail to recognize the changing seasons and fail to respond appropriately, we will be like a man sweating under a parka while water skiing on a summer lake, or like an alpine skier freezing in a swimsuit as he slaloms down a winter mountain slope.

One of the early references to the passing seasons of life is found in the Bible. The writer of the book of Ecclesiastes declares:

> There is a time for everything,
>   and a season for every activity under heaven:
>   a time to be born and a time to die,
>   a time to plant and a time to uproot,
>   a time to kill and a time to heal,
>   a time to tear down and a time to build,
>   a time to weep and a time to laugh,
>   a time to mourn and a time to dance,

a time to scatter stones and a time to gather them,
a time to embrace and a time to refrain,
a time to search and a time to give up,
a time to keep and a time to throw away,
a time to tear and a time to mend,
a time to be silent and a time to speak,
a time to love and a time to hate,
a time for war and a time for peace. (3:1–8)[1]

In short, the biblical writer tells us "timing is everything!" Change will come and we must adapt as quickly as possible. When we fail to change with the seasons, we run the risk of destroying relationships, missing creative opportunities, and stifling joy and laughter in life.

Some of us who watch American or Canadian football are fascinated with the timing and precision required in a hand-off between a quarterback and his running back. If the exchange is too quick, there is a real threat of a fumble and a good chance the blocking linemen will not have opened a "hole" for the running back to run through. He could just run into the pile of his own men and get nowhere. If the hand-off is too slow or the running back hesitates too long in the backfield, pathways opened by the linemen would begin to close again as the onrushing tacklers race in to throw the runner for a loss. To be successful in football, doing the right thing at the right time is all important.

Timing is important in marriage too. Knowing *when* to do something is almost as important as knowing *what* to do. I have been amazed at how many of my clients have entered marriage counseling with a poor sense of timing. One partner has made repeated attempts to revitalize the relationship, while the other largely ignores the signs of disquiet and despair in his or her spouse. Then, just when one partner quits trying and files for divorce, the spouse "wakes up" and wants to work at the marriage. Every counselor and pastor has had this type of couple in for counsel. Many of us have wished that both parties would have been more sensitive to the issue of timing. Divorce in cases such as this is the result of doing too little too late.

To get a better understanding of the relationship between life transitions and role conflict in marriage, we need to look at the problem of divorce from a developmental perspective.

Signs of Change

The idea of predictable crises in our lives is not new. In the mid seventies and early eighties, the concept of specific life transitions in the adult life cycle was popularized in Gail Sheehy's bestselling books *Passages* and *Pathfinders.*[2]

In his book *The Seasons of a Man's Life,*[3] Professor Daniel J. Levinson of Yale University reported on a four-year study of male development, concluding that men go through predictable emotional crises at certain chronological gate points in adult life. Both these authors drew much of their understanding of personality from the seminal works of Harvard Professor Erik Erikson and his research on the psychosocial development of clients.[4]

Levinson developed a chronological chart of significant times for each stage of development and the times for transitions between stages in the adult life cycle. Through the chart, Levinson graphically portrays the novice stage of entering the adult world in the twenties, the need to settle down in the thirties, the adjustment of one's expectations about life in the forties, and the task of planning for personal growth and enrichment in the fifties.[5] He proposes that we look at individuals chronologically, viewing them as negotiating certain developmental tasks within predictable periods of their lives. His study, focused on men only, (although a parallel study of women is in progress) largely addressed the span of from thirty to fifty years of age.

Naomi Golan, in her book *Passing Through Transitions,* synthesized Levinson's chronology, suggesting the following timetable which allowed for overlapping years, to accommodate premature and latent stage development:

Transition to Early Adult Years	18–22
Early Adulthood	22–40
Transition to Mid-Adult Years	38–42
Mid-Adulthood	42–62
Transition to Late Adult Years	60–65
Late Adulthood	65–85+[6]

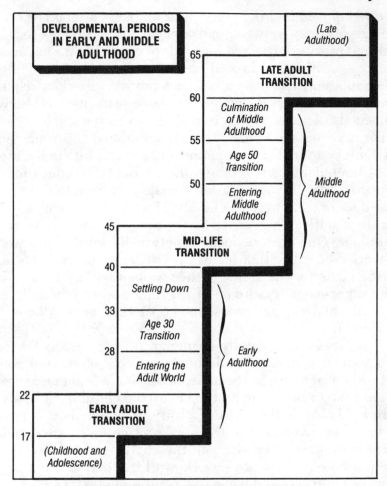

DEVELOPMENTAL PERIODS IN ADULT LIFE SPAN

Both Naomi Golan and Gail Sheehy attempted to broaden the investigation beyond midlife and included women in their studies.

Role Adjustment

Developmental psychologists inform us that chronology plays a significant role in the social and emotional adjustment of individuals. When two people marry, a number of factors come into play that are simply the result of one person's being at one stage of development and the other person's being at another stage. An age disparity between partners can compound the marital task and provide fertile soil for seeds of discord to sprout, as one spouse's emotional and social needs compete with those of the other spouse. Even when a husband and wife are relatively the same age and at approximately the same maturity level, developmental tasks may be different along sexual lines.

For a young adult male in early adulthood, his immediate task will be to find an occupation and support his family, often on a limited budget with significant debt for education or housing costs. The young adult female may have to forego career development to start a family. Her range of social activity may be significantly reduced by the time required in caring for an infant. One partner focuses outwardly toward the world of work while the other focuses inwardly on providing a nurturing home for the family. Other women will be involved in the "super-mom" syndrome of juggling a work schedule, day care of children, and maintenance of the couple's home or apartment.

This, however, is rapidly changing, as role models for men and women challenge traditional concepts of marital roles. "Mr. Mom" may not be the male model, but it is not uncommon to see a father balancing his time to attend childbirth classes or care for a baby in the midst of a busy work schedule. Women, in turn, are remaining in the marketplace, even after giving birth to children. They face all the challenges and stresses of their spouse's competitive work world, while attempting to manage child care and home life. Couples in this stage of early marriage may be left exhausted on evenings and weekends from their efforts to balance their personal and vocational lives.

With the passage of time, many marriages become characterized by a certain individualization and growing separateness. Couples often develop a parallel relationship where they share out of the same cupboard and sleep in the same bed, but for the most part, have very little in common. This alone contributes to the isolation and discontent often found in marriages on their way to divorce.

Vocational Conflicts

Vocational demands further complicate marital relationships. Corporations frequently uproot families for the sake of career development. Couples lose the support of extended family in such moves and spouses' energies are drained as the competitive tempo is escalated to achieve corporate goals. For the two-career marriage, such changes will force one spouse to surrender a job or perhaps a career, or walk the tightrope of maintaining two careers separated by many miles. Other businesses and occupations may not demand geographical change, but they still require a high level of career commitment. Many employers will expect a person's job to be his or her highest priority.

Levinson characterizes the twenties as a time when "a man is a 'novice' or 'apprentice' adult."[7] Couples in this period of development want to make a mark in life, to feel significant, to be considered "adult" in the autonomous sense of the term. Levinson views the latter half of early adulthood (32–40) in terms of two major tasks:

Task 1. To establish one's niche in society.
Task 2. To work at advancement.[8]

The result of such a developmental agenda forces many men to neglect nurturing relationships with family and friends and become very competitive and superficial in their interpersonal ties. Any commitments that stand in the way of vocational or career success tend to be jettisoned in order to achieve power or financial security. Many marriages begin to die during this stage as men and women lose their romantic excitement for each other and settle into a deadly parallelism. In some ways this is a very narcissistic phase: Men sacrifice all they have to the "god of success," neglecting to nourish familial relationships in the process.

While serving in the navy, I was saddened to see how many service personnel terminated their marriages when the choice came down to career or home. Heavy operational commitments, long absences from home, constant moves, and ever-existing danger in some jobs all mitigated against intimacy. Yet in spite of this, the aphrodisiac of power, prestige, pay, and pension kept many in the arms of the military long after their personal lives were destroyed. In essence, some service personnel I observed experienced divorces because they had an "extramarital affair" with the military. Their spouses no longer were willing to put up with such a triangulated relationship. This picture is similar to civilian counterparts in corporate life. A recent book, *The Military Family*, discusses the military man with this "corporate mentality." The writers see such a man as married to his work, causing his family to suffer:

> One discouraging thing we have learned in doing family therapy is the extent to which men reduce the family tension by leaving the family circle! Often such men have no inner life. They have never been intimate with anyone and unfortunately may never achieve closeness with anyone.[9]

The picture of a man entering midlife is one of someone who has made numerous personal sacrifices to be considered a senior member in his profession or trade. Concurrent with this drive for status and respect, many of these men experience an ever-diminishing inner life. Their lives are characterized by an increasing number of superficial, parasitic relationships which do little to help deal with the loneliness and meaninglessness of life. This is especially a problem for those who have made the supreme sacrifice for career or corporation and have lost family and friends in the process. The very people who could give meaning to one's work are no longer there. This loss dramatically impacts one's capability and motivation to do a good job.

Gail Sheehy, in looking at women approaching midlife, saw them attempting to move back into the work world in their thirties. Caregiving and homemaking were being forsaken for economic and emotional rewards found in the marketplace.

> The majority of caregivers found that even though their marriages may have been good, it wasn't enough. Nearly two thirds of them have now gone back to school or sought

jobs. . . . of that two thirds, seven made the move at age 30, fourteen at age 35, and the largest number, 35, at the age of 40.[10]

Yet in the midst of this change is a lot of risk and threat in marriage as roles change and the division of labor is altered in the home. If a husband married someone primarily to "keep the home fires burning" while he acted as provider, that relationship will be severely tested as the man and woman move toward midlife. Sheehy notes that "probably the caregiver's greatest fear is of being dumped. But there also is the fear of progressive vegetation. Frequently, the conflict between safety and autonomy does not come to a head until mid-life."[11] Unless a couple is flexible enough to negotiate new roles and relationships in each passage of time, they become vulnerable to a spiritual disease that could terminate their marriage.

MIDLIFE CHANGES

Age forty, which marks the beginning of the midlife transition, is usually greeted with a mixture of humor and negativism. Jack Benny's continual reference to only being thirty-nine when everyone knew he was well past sixty years old has become typical of our attitude toward aging. References to forty years of age and beyond are laced with comments about being "over the hill" or "past one's prime." In truth, some significant changes take place for couples around this middle-age transition time of life: physical concerns, psychological concerns, social matters, and vocational issues.

Physical Concerns

Health begins to deteriorate in the middle years; among the changes that concern these people the most are poor body tone and weight gain. Health clubs make a fortune off this group of people as they try to run off and exercise away the pounds. Plastic surgeons do their part, with face lifts, tummy tucks, and breast implants for the "over-the-hill gang." And the clothing industry specializes in "Big and Tall" or "Pretty and Plump" clothing outlets to accommodate those who lose "the battle of the bulge." We middle-agers think that we are beginning to see the end of the road up ahead. Our bodies are telling us that we are not going to live forever.

Psychological Concerns

The midlife transition is largely an existential crisis, with men and women evaluating past accomplishments and questioning the meaning of life. At one level this is a deeply spiritual moment, as a person inventories his or her life by an individual scale of values. "For many reasons . . . at 40 a man knows more deeply than ever before that he is going to die," says Sheehy. "He feels it in his bones, in his dreams, in the marrow of his being. His death is not simply an abstract, hypothetical event . . . at midlife, the growing recognition of mortality collides with the powerful wish for immortality and the many illusions that help maintain it."[12] From what we understand, both sexes experience existential discomfort at this time over the results of earlier choices.

How one has structured his or her life to this point can be very disquieting. Levinson says:

> It becomes important to ask: What have I accomplished? What do I get that really matters from my wife, children, friends, work, community and self? What is it that I truly desire for myself and others? What are my highest values and how are they reflected in my life? What are my greatest talents and how am I using (or wasting) them? What have I done with my early Dream and how can I adjust it now? Can I live in a way that combines my desires, values, and talents? How satisfactory is my present life structure—how suitable for me, how viable in the world—and how shall I change to provide a better basis for the future?[13]

All these concerns may not be formally asked, but the underlying anxiety and question will be there. Persons are looking at their successes and failures and facing their limitations. It is time to readjust the dreams and expectations of earlier years, to mourn the past and shape the future. The real issue is to try to find a sense of balance to life after the unbalanced life of the thirties.

For couples in this period, nothing is left unquestioned, including the marriage. Some couples may realize the foundation of their relationship was flawed from the beginning. Gary Collins, in writing about marriage at midlife, states:

> Middle age . . . can be a stage of life when there is unusual marital stress. Bored with the family routines of middle life, well aware of the weaknesses of one's mate, no longer held together by dependent children, and tired of routine sex, many middle-aged husbands and wives conclude that their marriages are in a state of instability and marital mid-life crises. Often there is a decline in intimacy, similarity of interest, and ability to communicate. As a result, the couple may resign themselves to marital boredom, decide on divorce, or find that one (or both) of the partners has slipped into a mid-life affair.[14]

There is an urgency to these issues that must be resolved. Ignoring them will not make them go away. On many of these relational issues no decision really *is* a decision to let the marriage die!

Social Concerns

Socially, many middle-aged couples long for deeper roots in society. In our mobile corporate world, there is little time to give oneself to anyone or any organization besides one's employer. This one-dimensional lifestyle leaves middle-aged adults with a lot of associates, but few friends. When I reflect on my life in the navy, I can remember how quickly we forgot and were forgotten within the first year of leaving one military assignment for another. By the second year, our Christmas-card list was modified significantly for the following year. Outside of a few special friendships, most relationships died in the changing circumstances. For many middle-aged couples loneliness is becoming a chronic problem. Very few couples can even count on one hand five people whom they could call for help in the midst of trouble. For partners who divorce in this stage of life, the shock is often severe because of a lack of friends and communal support to see them through the grieving process.

Vocational Concerns

Vocationally, midlife is different for men and women. For men, a sense of disillusionment seems to set in regarding their work. Either they have never really "made it" in the sense of acquiring all the power, perks, or money they had hoped for by midlife, or they achieved their goals only to discover they were not so important after all. A life lived on the ladder of success is precarious at best: If you don't get knocked off on the way up, when you get on top you risk continued attempts by younger men to push you off and take your place. The world of work thus becomes a dangerous place for a person who would like to be collegial rather than competitive.

Many vocational structures have only a few senior positions at the top. In these work situations most people will not make it to the top and are doomed to be by-passed at some point. The emotional effect of such "passovers" is devastating to the worker and sobering to fellow employees. While I was in the military, I would observe officers who were passed over. They were either constantly depressed and lethargic or always angry and irritable. Neither type of person was able to adjust easily to the rejection and humiliation of not being selected for increased responsibility in this competitive organization. You could count on a dramatic drop in the quality and quantity of the work of such a person. Others would often joke that the person had "retired on active duty," though still on the payroll for six to eight more years. Inherent in this situation is a feeling of having been devalued and unappreciated. For such a person, the middle-adult task will be to find ways of "sticking it out" until retirement or take risks on a new direction of life. Unemployment in middle adulthood can be devastating. The world of work confers upon a man his primary value in society. When that work is taken from him, he loses self-esteem and feels he has lost his manhood. Many divorces occur among the unemployed for this reason. Without a sense of value and purpose, people find it hard to keep getting up in the morning to look for work. Such a man "loses face" among his peers, within his family, and especially with his wife—unless she is committed to him. Alcoholism or suicide appears to be a solution to the intense psychic pain of rejection.

Women respond to midlife in a somewhat different manner. For many, the twenties and early thirties represented a time of care-giving and nurturing of children. When the children leave home, and husbands are absorbed in their careers, many wives go back to school or rejoin the work force. The energy with which they throw themselves into their new-found careers or education can be surprising. They seem to be trying to make up for lost time. In many cases they forsake some of their nurturing roles to shift energy to their own professional development. Not uncommonly, in their early forties men recognize they have neglected the relational and emotional side of life only to find the wife has new interests.

"In some families, the wife's growing assertiveness and freedom are accompanied by the husband's severe decline," notes Levinson. "He has less authority and involvement in family life and feels increasingly obsolescent at work. When this occurs, it is a serious problem for the entire family."[15] If there is ever a time when a couple is most likely to be out of step with each other, it is during the early to mid-forties. If they can somehow negotiate these issues during these years and get to the late forties or early fifties, things often improve relationally. Midlife may be painful, but it passes.

THE ADJUSTMENT TO CHANGING SEASONS

Adjustments become more difficult as one grows older. "You can't teach an old dog new tricks" we say. When we were younger we enjoyed variety and change; there was something exhilarating about trying new things. However, the older we become the less enthusiastic we may be about change. Most like life to be predictable and orderly. We don't like surprises (except at Christmastime or birthdays). Even when things are bad, we often refuse to change: We doubt our capacity for making good decisions or we dislike the negative possibilities of our risk taking.

Counselors need to encourage risk taking from time to time.

In order for people to take some risks to change their circumstances, they need to be able to renounce one life to grasp another. Paul Tournier writes ". . . there is always in life a place to leave and a new place to find, and in between a zone of hesitation and uncertainty tinged with more or less intense anxiety. . . . there is a past security to be lost before we find a new security."[16]

Spiritual Adjustments

The first step in dealing with the difficulty of transitioning involves helping counselees commit the situation to a wise and sovereign God. Prayer and meditation need to focus on seeking God's grace so that we hear and act upon his will in the midst of our relationships. This will involve encouraging counselees to depend upon the Lord to help them be flexible on issues that scare them.

I have a picture in mind that I want to paint someday. The idea for the painting came from rereading the story of Abraham and it concerns his faith in the middle of transitions. In my mental picture Abraham is standing upon a hill looking toward the promised land. God has just ordered him to venture into the unknown. All he can see is the fertile green pastureland on which he stands, a verdant scene that gradually turns to desert in the distance. Before him, not more than a thousand yards away, the land appears as a gray haze. Behind him, he sees the tents of his family and friends, and a cool stream running through the valley. He sees Sarah hanging out the laundry on the tent lines, his friends getting ready for a night of conversation and games around the campfire, and his cattle and sheep enjoying ample supplies of water and grass. Life is so content here, so predictable, so safe, he seems to be saying. Yet his spirit has become disquieted as he feels the nudge of God upon his life.

I can imagine him going down into the camp and telling Sarah to pack up because they would be leaving at first light; and I can see the quizzical look she gives him. Abraham announces to his friends he is leaving in the morning, and when asked where he is going, all he can answer is, "I don't know." I don't believe he made those first steps—that big transition—"whistling a happy tune." I can almost hear his friends telling each other that he is crazy. And Sarah possibly is saying, "Abe, I sure hope you heard the Lord right and that you weren't just hallucinating after being out in the sun too long."

I learn from that bit of sanctified imagining that faith is not so much the absence of questions and doubt, but an obedience to walk, and to keep walking, God's way in the midst of questions, criticism, and doubt. That is what made Abraham the "father of faith" and the patron saint of all who have to make life transitions. We need to share with those we counsel that the same God of Abraham, Isaac, and Jacob is still leading his people into their personal promised lands God has prepared.

Emotional Adjustments

The second step is to identify basic truths about midlife and adjust emotionally to what is developing. Jerry and Mary White, writing in *The Christian in Mid-Life*, list four facts about midlife we should consider:

1. In mid-life there will be role changes and reversals especially in the areas of leadership, material needs, and spiritual matters.
2. The greatest failure in mid-life is the failure to realize that we have both changed and will keep changing.
3. A growing independence can lead to selfishness.
4. Failure to aggressively deepen and strengthen a marriage in the midst of differences and conflict will make it more vulnerable to divorce.[17]

Emotionally, midlife brings mixed feelings as couples go through a season of questions, evaluating their past and future. Mood shifts are common and spouses should be aware of the need for their partners to sort things out. This phase cannot be rushed, but must take its course as each person resolves his or her inner conflict.

Relational Adjustments

The third step is to work to recreate intimacy. This may involve the formal intervention of a counselor or referral to one of the marriage enrichment/encounter programs.

In one survey, couples were asked to define intimacy and how they experienced it. They reported the following:

"Intimacy is knowing there's someone who cares about the children as much as you do."

"Intimacy is a history of shared experience."

"It's sitting there having a cup of coffee together and watching the eleven-o'clock news."

"It's knowing you care about the same things."

"It's knowing she'll always understand."

"It's him sitting in the hospital for hours at a time when I was sick."

"It's knowing he cares when I'm hurting."

"It's standing by me when I was out of work."

"It's seeing each other at our worst."

"It's sitting across the breakfast table."

"It's talking when you're in the bathroom."

"It's knowing we'll begin and end each day together."[18]

Notice the common, everyday quality of the circumstances that enhance intimacy. It doesn't cost a lot to take time out for coffee or a walk in the evening. Couples don't have to take expensive vacations to restore intimacy. It is, instead, a matter of focus and priorities linked with a positive, collaborative attitude which will lead to real togetherness. Counselors can assist people by assigning "homework" that suggests taking time out for the ordinary disciplines of life that bring two individuals together and encourage them to think and feel in terms of "us" and "we" again.

Priority Adjustment

The fourth step is to encourage couples to reorder their priorities to care for one another better. This involves having a "growth plan" for one another. It suggests they creatively brainstorm together about each other's gifts and graces. This can lead to adopting a strategy to help them stretch and grow in areas of need and is best done in the context of a caring community that supports and encourages change. Without such a group, it is difficult to achieve lasting change. We need to help counselees take care of themselves mentally, physically, and spiritually. Regular exercise, weight control, listening to music, prayer and meditation, cultivating a hobby, and socializing with intimate friends are all nourishing activities. In order to reduce stress couples need occasional "time outs," such as long weekends away from home or evenings out on a date.

As counselors we help people take responsibility for their lives, so that they act, rather than react. It is important to communicate to couples that they can't have it both ways. Either they commit more time and resources to their relationship and enjoy new vigor and life there, or they give away their energy to other causes and expect a deteriorating marital relationship. Resources spent in one domain are not available to be spent elsewhere. Each couple has to make a choice!

Couples can spend a little time each week maintaining their relationship. By doing so, problematic trends are caught before they become crises.

INTERVENTION STRATEGIES

Counselors are faced with significant developmental issues in dealing with divorce in middle age. The biggest enemy is a sense of hopelessness and despair that is inherent in long-neglected relationships. It is not enough to eliminate symptomatic behavior (i.e., alcoholism or extramarital affairs); we must address the boredom and sense of claustrophobia that often characterize marriage relationships at this life stage. This is a time when opportunity exists for pastoral intervention in many people's lives. A midlife marriage enrichment program may be a nonthreatening way of introducing such pastoral care. Home visitation programs or home evening programs for family may be helpful also.

Pointing out to clients some reasons for their spouses' behavior will require skill, as will the design of coping strategies to help them adjust to change. In some cases, extensive career guidance and personality testing may be in order, to help people make intelligent choices. Counselors need to empower couples to negotiate conflicted passages of their lives through a guided discussion of goals and values, and communication skills exercises.

In many cases, a cocounseling team is an ideal way to address the issues husbands and wives experience in life transition. When a divorce follows a life transition, it is important to marshal community and church resources to care for those shattered by the experience. Often the sense of failure is so intense that some people may even attempt suicide as a manipulative means to rescue the marriage.

Time does not need to be an enemy, but rather a friend. It is something to be embraced and enjoyed, not to be wasted or avoided. It is important that we remember—and share this truth with counselees: If we are in Christ we live forever! The seasons will come and go and we will change, but we will continue to *Be!*

Ministry in the seasons of life ultimately deals with life-and-death-issues—concerns for meaning and purpose in the light of death. If counselors can bring faith and hope in the midst of this concern, they will have done a great work.

CHAPTER TEN

DIVORCE AND THE MINISTRY

HOW CAN WE HELP THE HELPERS?

Unfolding a Christmas newsletter, I began reading of the painful parting of a fellow navy chaplain and his wife, and I was grieved with the news. For several weeks I walked around depressed, finding it very difficult to focus on my own ministry. I felt torn in my loyalties, for they were both friends. I did not fully understand what had happened. They were both very caring and competent people. Somehow something pretty drastic must have happened to end this seventeen-year marriage.

At one time this family could have been pictured in some advertising brochure to recruit seminarians for the military chaplaincy. Outwardly they were the model couple, attractive people who said the right things and did the right things. They were gifted people, exercising these talents to touch many peoples' lives. Now my friend's ex-wife is a single parent with two teenage children, trying, with the loving help of a church family, to put her life back together again. My friend, and former colleague, left the ministry and has moved to another city to start over again. Probably this experience more than anything else has prompted me to risk writing on this subject (knowing many clergy may not understand). This chapter describes the *male* pastor, since most pastors are men, but the writer does realize that women are serving in the pastorate as well.

According to an article in *Leadership* magazine:

> More and more ministers are getting divorced. One recent survey of divorce rates by profession found ministers with the third highest rate, behind only medical doctors and policemen. Other indicators on the survey suggest that the only reason ministers are not the most divorced is because many, for theological reasons, stick with tough marriages most would abandon.[1]

One of the ministers participating in the magazine interview is quoted as saying: "I could count twenty-five pastors in our singles ministry as recently as six months ago."[2]

The church is being faced with a significant problem in the way we select, train, deploy, and support people in Christian ministry. With all of our emphasis on task orientation and mission, it is so easy to neglect the needs of the people who are involved in the work of the ministry. Yet, I believe there are a lot of "hurting helpers" out in the ministry. This not only includes pastors, but missionaries, church and mission executives, Bible college and seminary professors, Christian counselors, military and hospital chaplains, and many others involved vocationally in church or parachurch ministries. Attendant with such a listing is a concern for the "forgotten family"—the family who stands behind every one of these individuals involved in Christian vocation.

I would like to look at this issue of divorce in the parsonage in an attempt to help fellow pastors care for one another, to help counselors in their understanding of this unique group of people, and to help church leaders design better pastoral-care systems for their clergy. Primarily, I wish to focus on the problems encountered by pastors and their families and then look at some possibilities for ministry to them.

THE PROBLEM WITH PASTORS

Problems are not unique to the Christian life; but, rather, they come with being human and living in a fallen world. Pastors and their wives are no different in many respects from other people. They all have a psychic history with differing degrees of neurosis from the push and shove of life. Some pastors are emotionally balanced people, interested in ministering to others, while taking proper care of themselves and those they love. But some have low self-esteem and need constant affirmation. Others have a craving need for power and control, feeling very insecure and inferior about their lives, while still others have a narcissistic need to be "the life of the party," seeking center stage as a means of confirming to themselves that they are valuable.

Pastors and their wives have grown up in a variety of environments. Some came from poor homes and may have struggled in their adult years with issues related to financial security in a career which generally pays poorly. Others came from backgrounds of more affluence. They may have seen power as a predominant goal. Some grew up in homes where parents were loving and the marriage remained intact. Others spent their formative years listening to parents argue or experiencing physical or mental abuse. Some grew up in homes where insecurity reigned because of their parents' alcohol or drug abuse. Still others grew up experiencing the divorce of parents and have struggled for years with issues of love and loyalty, especially where stepfamily relationships added confusion.

Pastors and their wives have also grown up with a variety of religious experiences. Some were raised in homes where they learned that God loved them and they saw his grace lived out in their home and church. Others grew up seeing God as angry and wrathful; they have lived with fear and legalism. Many selected life partners who are embittered as a result of growing up in such environments. Some know the church as a caring, affirming community, while others see it as a place where you obey a list of rules and suffer painful rejection when those rules are broken. All of us, as human beings, struggle with scars of the past, frustrations with the present, and fear of the future. We all sense that time is inexorably dragging us through life cycles which culminate in death. What, then, makes the life of someone in ministry different from anyone else? I would like to look at some unique issues in the pastor's role, the pastor's call, and the pastor's family.

The Pastor's Role

I can remember going to my first pastorate as a "wet-behind-the-ears" seminary graduate. I was armed with three years of class notes on courses in Old Testament, New Testament, biblical languages, systematic theology, Christian education, and practical theology. I was a walking reservoir of knowledge about God, looking for a place to dump that information. Yet nothing in seminary had prepared me for the practical aspects of ministry which I confronted.

My first clue that something was missing in my training was the advice of a "practical" theology professor regarding living in a parsonage next to the church. He told the class that if such a situation existed upon their arrival at a new church, the pastor was to convene a board meeting and tell the church he refuses to live in the parsonage and suggests they can rent it out to someone else.

"Never," he said, "live in a parsonage next to the church!"

To my chagrin, my first church did have a parsonage, which not only sat right next to the church, but it had an attached garage converted into a fellowship hall with Sunday school classrooms in the basement. I intuitively figured out it would not be politically wise to put up a fuss on the first day (though we later came to appreciate why that professor warned of such an arrangement). In any case, armed with such impractical theology I began my ministry. The people were loving and caring, enduring the task placed upon many small churches—namely, to "grow another pastor" for the denomination. I knew nothing about building programs or fund raising to support these efforts. Yet, there I was, a pastor of a newly constructed church, with hardly anyone attending. Without ever having had a course on church budgets, fund raising, recruitment of volunteers, evangelism, church growth and church planting, community building, or management, I deduced I was expected to fill the church up quickly before it went under financially. All this was to be done on a salary of $60.00 a week (with house and utilities) plus some fresh vegetables from parishioners' gardens and an occasional rabbit or pheasant from hunters in the congregation.

During the five years we ministered there, three sons were born into our home, while we both held down part-time jobs to make ends meet. Yet God met us there, and by trial and error Judy and I began to learn our roles as "the pastor" and "the pastor's wife."

The people-relating skills we learned were helpful, as were the rich experiences of ministering to diverse but caring people. The masking of our true feelings that we learned and the futile attempts "to be all things to all people" were harmful. When we left our first church, we left with a mixture of feelings that have taken years to sort out. I recognize now, eighteen years later, how overwhelmed I felt as a twenty-four-year-old being initiated into the ministry.

Pastors have no need to hear such a story; probably many could tell a better one! They have lived it and know what I describe is largely true in American church life (though the multiple-staff situation may not be fraught with the same type of problems; the politics, power, and personality issues of being the junior-most member of the staff is just as frustrating).

At their source, many problems in the parsonage start with role confusion for the pastoral couple (I recognize there are unmarried clergy who experience some of the same problems, but I am seeking to show a linkage between pastoral pressures and problems in clergy marriages.) The expectations of pastors and their wives are often very different from those of their congregation. Edward Bratcher, writing in *The Walk-on-Water Syndrome* states: ". . . the pastor is expected to walk on water and he cannot, and he becomes angry with himself because he cannot. . . ."[3] He goes on to list some of the expectations the average congregation has of its pastor:

(1) He must be a perfect moral example.
(2) He must provide moral and emotional support at all times regardless of his own condition.
(3) He must be an able administrator, both in the church and in the community.
(4) He must be an able public speaker on any and every topic.
(5) He must perform as an actor—keep people on the edge of their seats at all times, be able to act in all settings (i.e., funerals, weddings, picnics, baptisms, etc.).
(6) He must serve as a philosopher—a teacher of values— even though the people agree beforehand that they will not listen.
(7) He must perform as a counselor, a role which is particularly emotionally exhausting.[4]

Obviously, several themes leap out as we read such a list. The job description is actually designed for a superman. By its very nature, like housework to the housewife, the pastor's job is never done. It carries with it a moral imperative ("must") and is laced with absolute terms like "be perfect," "be able," "act always." This list (a short one at that) programs a pastor to failure. When he can't measure up, he will try to cover-up by blaming others, or blow up by blaming himself.

In the first situation, this leads to conflict in the church and isolation and loneliness for the pastor and his wife. In the second situation, this leads to conflict in the home or depressive/withdrawing behavior. In both cases, the pastoral family quickly "circles the wagons" to defend themselves against the real or imagined criticisms of church members and denominational superiors. It is no wonder pastoral families are some of the loneliest people in town. This defensive posture explains why it is often so difficult to counsel pastors and their wives. They are suspicious of outsiders who are trained in the "dark art" of secular psychology (even Christian therapists have problems being accepted) and they are afraid to talk to other pastors and their wives (the competition) or conference superintendents (who have the capability of relieving them or demoting them). They are trapped in a vicious cycle where they either hold in their anger and frustration (taking the form of somatic problems or depression) or explode at other people (taking the form of church fights or family violence). Extreme forms of destructive behavior include spouse and child abuse, alcoholism, or sexual addiction. Though problems in many pastoral homes may not be at the extremes mentioned, they are to some degree pathological.

There also is confusion regarding the ministry. The congregation may have one view while the pastor has another. He may want the church to be more biblically and theologically literate, involved in evangelism and socially active in the community. He desires the church to be inclusive rather than an exclusive community of believers. The pastor may see the members of the church as fellow ministers in the proclamation of the gospel. The church, however, may buy into the clergy-laity dichotomy, delegating the "work of the ministry" to the pastor. They may view him as "their hired man," their religious surrogate to represent their faith to the community. They may be more interested in a nicer sanctuary or a larger fellowship hall or gymnasium to make life more comfortable (certainly such investments can expand the ministry positively). The idea of personal outreach (other than financial contribution to the institution to support the pastoral staff and program) is foreign to many congregations. The priesthood of all believers is a nice sounding Reformation concept, but, in truth, is resisted by both clergy and church members for different reasons. Clergy don't want to give up power, but want to retain complaining rights over working too hard. People in the pew feel untrained for the work of the ministry and are laden with a lot of responsibilities from their own professions. In short, the pastor and the congregation may be on a collision course for conflict over unrealistic expectations about what each other's role should be in the ministry. Again, pastors bring home their frustration over the death of their ideals. Since there is no one else to listen to the pastor, the spouse is trapped, carrying the whole weight of disillusionment upon her or his shoulders. The reasons that challenged them to enter the ministry come into conflict with the vision, or lack thereof, of their supporting, employing congregation.

The Pastor's Spouse's Role

Pastoral spouses also are confused over role and function in the ministry. Whether they like it or not, they have stepped into "a way of life" rather than just an occupation. In one sense they do not have a job (i.e., get paid for specific tasks), yet in another sense, an unwritten job description awaits the "pastor's wife." Since nothing is written down, the gift of mind reading is essential. Usually this means most or all of the following:

(1) Attend all services (in sickness and in health).
(2) Be a good hostess for the congregation.
(3) Accompany pastoral spouse in home and hospital visitation.
(4) Teach or assist in the religious education program.
(5) If musical, participate in church musical programs.
(6) Be available to plan and attend church picnics, socials, or community affairs (which means work outside the home must be limited).
(7) Be a role model of discretion and godliness.
(8) Enthusiastically support the ministry of one's spouse and the goals of the church.

Again, we see a "job description" that could be entitled "A Never Ending Story." It calls for the wife to be vocationally ambidextrous and socially sophisticated. She is to exude glowing support and good cheer from the pew. In a sense she is the closest thing the church has to a cheerleader. This is not to say that all pastors' wives wish to live up to these expectations. Some are self-assured enough to focus their efforts and set parameters around their time, particularly if they have young children who need their attention.

David and Vera Mace, leading international authorities in the field of marriage counseling, write about a study they performed with clergy couples dealing with marital satisfaction. Stating their findings concerning the frustrations of pastors' wives, they say:

Prominently at the top of the list is the need for "time alone together." Two thirds of the wives have checked this. . . .

Half the wives are confused about just what they are expected to do. . . . Friendships outside the church have also been a perplexing matter for clergy wives, and inevitably this is linked with the question of taking an outside job. The issue of privacy, or lack of it, in the pastor's family life can be counted on to come up again and again. It is linked mainly with the parsonage system. . . . We get a disturbing picture of the clergy wife carrying a heavy load. Denied adequate time for maintaining the intimate relationship with her husband, she often feels lonely and frustrated. . . . Add all this together, and we begin to understand why she has so much difficulty handling her negative emotions.[5]

The cry for intimacy in the parsonage is of vital concern for anyone concerned with helping clergy marriages remain healthy. Home should be a sanctuary where ministry couples can "let down their hair" and be themselves. (I'm not advocating a fortress mentality as much as I am calling for a private component in every couple's life to remain emotionally healthy.) Boundaries between public life and personal life must be established and maintained in the parsonage. The "glass house" can have a damaging effect on clergy marriages over a period of time unless such boundaries are recognized and honored. There is a time to shut the door and unplug the phone. Without such time, the clergy couple has little to give to anyone else.

One of the biggest problems in public ministry and clergy marriages is the "messiah complex" of many ministers. This closet workaholism (spiritualized as "I'd rather burn out for Jesus than rust out") is encouraged by many task-oriented religious organizations. Pastors with low self-esteem, inferiority complexes and power or control needs will spend hours doing church work since they get affirmation for their sacrificial attitude. Meanwhile, family concerns are neglected because there are no medals given for many of the repetitive chores found in maintaining a family. Responsibility is expected in the home and rarely rewarded. Only when something is forgotten is performance duly noted—and then the critique is negative. Only when the family starts acting out (depressive or drug-dependent spouse, promiscuous/alcoholic daughter, vandalizing son) do many clergy realize the cost for such inattentive family living. Even then, however, a lot of energy is focused at controlling behavior (in the early stages of disintegration) and blaming or scapegoating (in the later stages of dysfunction). At root is the fear of job loss and status loss, since tremendous pressure exists for the clergy persons and their families to be good role models for the congregation to the community.

Several years ago, I found myself in an assignment doing pastoral counseling in a Navy-Marine Corps Family Service Center in Okinawa, Japan. All day long I saw clients dealing with marital/situational stress. I conducted family-life education seminars, cofacilitated a weekly spouse-abuse group, preached in chapel on Sunday and, in my "spare time," taught in the graduate school for the University of Maryland—Far East Division. As a "hobby" I began work on my doctoral dissertation. Not surprisingly, I began to develop chest pains, which after extensive medical evaluation proved to be "nonspecific" (a medical euphemism for an illness my father would have said was all in my head!). This experience forced me to take a good look at my life and ask myself, "what is driving me to work at such a killing pace?" Only as I began to look at my deep need for affirmation was I able to gain some control of my work schedule and "return" to my family. I took time out for exercise, devotional times, long sunset walks with my wife and playing ball with my sons. These activities restored balance in my life. I found I did a better job. When tempted to pick up old habits, I remember my doctor saying to me: "You can take some time off now or later. Today it is your choice; tomorrow it will be mine (i.e., with me lying in bed in a cardiac ward) or the undertaker's (i.e., with me lying dead in a box in a grave)."

In many ways, ministerial workaholism is like a triangulated affair with the church, in which the pastor's wife dare not protest lest she be thought unspiritual. Some spousal anger among clergy wives is projected against God over the loss of their husbands to God's work. There is a sense of despair and hurt with such wives, for they recognize they can't compete with something so big as God. Only the strongest wives can strip the spiritual veneer to confront the bare reality of neurotic behavior. At times, leaving the professional ministry for a season may be the only way for a clergy couple to get well. If this is in order, a lot of emotional support is needed to make this transition without the sense of failure that can accompany such a furlough.

Gordon McDonald calls for ministers and counselors to confront and challenge a number of heretical myths about the way we spend our time in ministry:

Myth 1. We are individually responsible for saving the whole world. . . .

Myth 2. Time is running out; too little of it is left.

Myth 3. A pastor needs to be constantly available for all emergencies. . . .

Myth 4. Rest, recreation, and leisure are second-class uses of time. . . .

Myth 5. It is glamorous, even heroic, to burn out, break down, and even relationally blow up if you can prove that your friend, your spouse, or your congregation left you because you were faithfully discharging your call. . . .

Myth 6. The family of the Christian leader automatically surrenders its right to spiritual and familial leadership by the father.[6]

Obviously we see how foolish these myths are, yet many Christian ministers functionally live at this level in their attempts to save the world.

The Pastor's Calling and Training

Serving in a Bible college I hear students talking about a "call" to missions or a "call" to the urban poor. Implied in these conversations is something mystical and awesome—God actually speaking to someone about going somewhere and doing something for him! This call is an unverifiable entity which must be accepted at face value. Yet, it is confusing to many people considering Christian service. I am convinced that many problems within the marriage of clergy persons and their ministries stem from misunderstanding this issue of calling. Many are not gifted pastorally and should never be involved in the unstructured multi-task environment of the pastorate or mission enterprise. What they heard as a "call" does not seem to be verified by performance or experience. "Calling," properly decoded, in many cases, is interpreted to mean that a portion of Scripture dealing with the Great Commission challenged their hearts and they volunteered to serve. For others it was a growing awareness of a need in a certain part of the world and they were responding on the basis of the biblical principle to "love [their] neighbor as oneself." For others, they were trained or gifted in a certain manner and it seemed reasonable, if the church needed volunteers for a tough task, to go and serve.

I believe we need to reevaluate our understanding of a lifelong career in full-time Christian service. Otherwise, Christians feel like soldiers deserting in the heat of the battle if they ever leave the ministry. If opportunities expand and God blesses what a person does, this may be a good indicator to stay on. In other cases, a short-term missionary experience may verify to a couple that they are not cut out for such service. They can return to the local church with a better appreciation of the worldwide ministry of the church. This way people can graciously move in and out of vocation in keeping with the needs of the church and their own needs. Gone would be the stigma attached to "leaving the ministry," which keeps many couples locked into situations they should have left much earlier. Candidates' "calling to ministry" should blend a sense of conviction and challenge from Scripture with a vision of human need, including their own need. Also necessary in this process is a confirmation and endorsement of an individual's call from a body of believers who have observed the candidate's gifts and graces over a period of time and recommend him or her for ministry.

This is what I believe the Bible means when it warns us: "Do not be hasty in the laying on of hands (for ordination) . . ." (1 Tim. 5:22). We may save more pastors and their wives a lot of grief and keep them from many wasted years with such a policy.

A number of years ago I heard about an ordination service in which the candidate tore up the ordination parchments after they were handed him and declared that such a presentation was inappropriate. Until church leaders took seriously their responsibility to observe him and his work, he felt their certification and endorsement of his ministry was meaningless. Denominational supervision and support are often inconsistent at best, and negligent at worst. The young minister and his wife can sense they are on the front lines alone. Pastoral care should be routinely provided for the pastoral family, preferably by someone other than the pastor's denominational supervisor. This could be arranged by regional appointment of a ministry couple skilled in listening to and helping young couples starting out in the ministry adjust to problems in the ministry. It also is essential for denominational leaders to support pastors and their wives in the midst of their ministry with frequent visits—encouraging, advising, and providing helpful insights. I remember a wise and gentle superintendent giving this sort of help to me in my early years of ministry.

The Pastor's Family

The struggle to carve out quality time for pastors and their families is one of the biggest problems in clergy marriages. Without time for one another, the pastor's family loses its sense of center, its sense of cohesiveness, which can carry the family through tough times. The storms can gather unthreateningly on the outside if a ministry family has a sense of warmth and intimacy on the inside.

I remember a time as a pastor when Judy and I were feeling driven to get involved in a particular church program for which we had little vision or enthusiasm. Yet, we knew that to refuse would bring the wrath of some key people upon our lives. We had a habit in the morning of taking a second cup of coffee together and just talking, reading Scripture, and praying at our kitchen table. Coincidentally, we started a Bible study on the book of Galatians. We were impressed with the apostle Paul's warning in Galatians 5:1: ". . . do not let yourselves be burdened again by a yoke of slavery." Suddenly it struck us that that was exactly what we were doing. We began to lovingly say no to some projects. Predictably, the storms came, but because of those special morning moments, we were "together" as a couple and had a sense of God's direction in our lives. Before, we had conformed to other people's agenda and had outward peace but inner conflict; now we had outward conflict but inner peace! Given the choice, I would choose the latter.

Family cohesiveness is essential for a healthy ministry. Roger Palms, editor of *Decision* magazine recommends that the pastor take leadership in the home and church in defeating the "time bandits" of endless committee meetings and social activities in the church.

> Very few clergy neglect family and home because they plan to; it happens slowly, and part of the reason it happens is that the most intimate relationships are not occurring at home, not because the ministers don't want them to, but because they have allowed the ministry to become a twenty-four hour job. We need to be quiet sometimes, relax sometimes, and be with our family. We do the congregation a great disservice if we do not show them that this is important for us and for them too. If we imply that our busyness is the "Christian way," they may praise us for hard work, but they will not learn that we have a responsibility to our families and that they do too.[7]

Time, as important as it is, is not enough, It must be *quality* time, dedicated to intimacy, open communication, and love. Every pastor is first a priest of his own home before he is a pastor to his people. The whole basis of his ordination rests upon his capability to manage both his family and ministerial responsibilities (1 Timothy 3:4–5). If he loses his credibility at home, he often loses it in the larger family of faith. Too many pastors have tried to save the world only to lose their families and their marriages in the process. God does not call us to such reckless relational living. We are called to live a balanced life: being loving to our mate, caring to our children, and a model to our people. That is a tall order for any pastor! We may ask: "Who is sufficient for these things?" Our Lord tells us: "My grace is sufficient for you, for my power is made perfect in weakness" (2 Cor. 12:9).

THE POSSIBILITIES FOR PASTORS

We can talk about problems and miss the positive aspects of ministry. Most people enter the ministry with altruistic motives. They believe that God's love is the greatest message in the world and they are excited about sharing it with others. Most people enter the ministry with a wide array of talents and a desire to further the gospel. Most ministry couples are more than willing to be involved in public ministry, to see lives changed through their efforts. They are in the ministry because they believe they are making a difference in the world. The pastor and his wife, however, need help in learning how to prevent a breakdown.

Prevention Plan

It has been said "an ounce of prevention is worth a pound of cure." We don't have to get sick to experience wholeness. We can take preventive measures to care for ourselves and avoid problems.

The couple in ministry can avoid personal burnout and marriage failure by taking the following steps:

1. Setting realistic goals[8]
2. Doing the same thing differently
3. Breaking away
4. Taking things less personally
5. Accentuating the positive
6. Changing jobs[9]

Couples can defeat loneliness by beginning to date again. Even the idea of "going out" when one or both of them are gone almost every evening seems strange. Yet there is a need for a change of scenery, a change of focus, and a change of conversation. Only as our lives have a sense of contrast and rhythm is there an excitement to living. This may involve a short getaway to a nice hotel for several days or daily routines like "table talk" with coffee, or walks together in the sunset—sharing one's hopes, dreams, and laughter together. Many couples have forgotten how to play. Play must become part of the life in the parsonage. Only with a sense of shared humor can the pastor and his wife face some of the struggles in their ministry.

Gordon McDonald, writing in *Restoring Your Spiritual Passion*, calls couples to a Sabbath rest:

Sabbath is God's antidote to workaholism. It is the check-mate to men and women who have fallen into the trap of believing that their personal worth is built upon what they do rather than what they are. . . . I like to refer to Sabbath as the still time, the special moment in my calendar. If the map of my life should be marked with frequent safe places, the calendar of my life should show Sabbaths or still times.[10]

It is important for pastors to use their calendars to schedule times of renewal and relationship with their wives. It will be the best divorce-prevention program available—and it only costs time!

Intervention Plan

What do we say to pastors and their wives who are broken by divorce? We start by offering them our love. We accept them as God accepts them—sinners saved by grace. We walk with them and work with them so they can recover emotionally and spiritually. This may mean regular times to get together, just to listen and hear the hurt and pain in their hearts. It may involve acting as a priest for them as they confess sin and seek forgiveness. It may mean advocacy, as we seek to restore a brother or sister to fellowship with God's people.

Practical issues will emerge in helping the divorced. Significant assistance will be required in locating new employment or educational opportunities for one or both partners (since in many churches the pastor loses his employment upon divorcing or being divorced and few ex-wives can live on nonexistent spousal/child support of someone unemployed). It may call for counseling, to work through psychological and spiritual conflicts. In time, ministry to the divorced may lead to reinvolvement in the life of the church. I do not believe there is justification for preventing divorced persons who have submitted to church discipline from ever serving the church in some capacity again. If, over a period of time, they show fruits of repentance and have demonstrated spiritual maturity, they should be able to share that experience with the body of Christ. The only biblical limitations on divorced persons seem to relate to bishops, elders, and deacons in the church (1 Tim. 3:1–2, 12). The rationale for that primarily is not to give occasion for reproach from people outside the church. Acceptance within the body of Christ should be expected, though ministry function may be limited.

Divorce in the ministry is a painful thing for the church and for the couple parting. No one is advocating or defending divorce in the parsonage. Not only do couples suffer, but so does the church. Divorce is a wound in the body of Christ which causes all to hurt. Individual lives are shattered and reproach is brought upon the Christian community. Divorce embarrassingly underlines that we have problems living with and loving one another. Yet two wrongs don't make a right. We do not need to add further insult to injury and demonstrate continued lovelessness in the face of tragedy. We don't always demonstrate perfection to the world, but we can show there is grace and love in the midst of brokenness in a fallen world. May the theme of our ministry be redemption rather than condemnation. May our aim be to help rather than to hurt the hurting.

LIFE AFTER DIVORCE

Several years ago my family and I were vacationing on the East Coast when we got lost. As we entered the outskirts of a large eastern city, we took a wrong turn. We drove endlessly, feeling confused and losing hope by the minute. We didn't dare to stop and ask directions because of the dangerous neighborhoods we were driving through. Only by accident we found our way out of that area to a place where we felt safe to get out and ask for help. We got directions, and soon we were back on the main road to our destination.

Divorce is often like that experience. It is hard to point out just where both partners went wrong. They know they did and this results in aimlessness, confusion, and hopelessness. Many find themselves in threatening circumstances which preclude asking directions. The fear and frustration many divorced persons feel cause them to despair of ever feeling good about their lives again.

I have tried to provide a roadmap for counselors and clergy which will help them make sense of a confusing situation. The aim throughout the book was to identify milestones and signposts along the way which pastoral counselors could use to identify problem areas and then guide couples out of the emotional wilderness of divorce.

Several things need to be said in summary regarding the issue of divorce and the divorcing. First, divorce involves sin. But it is not an unpardonable sin. Still, the consequences of divorce—like any sinful action—can be felt for years. This calls for counseling and a pastoral care that shows real concern, walking with people through seasons of conflict and confusion. The church encourages couples to honor their marriage commitments with consistency and care. When people fail in that endeavor, and the result is divorce, the church calls men and women to repentance, forgiveness, and reconciliation. When restoration is impossible, the church is called to help divorced people cope with the loneliness and difficulty of single parenting or perhaps the complex ethical and relational issues of remarriage and stepfamily living.

Second, pastors and counselors need to view the circumstances surrounding divorce with the bifocal lenses of faith. It's so easy to look down at the tangled, conflicted circumstances of life and see nothing which would offer hope and renewal. We want to look above those circumstances with lenses which clearly give us the long view of eternity and show us God's power and grace to renew broken lives. Only as we live in two dimensions—natural and supernatural—can we seek God's power to change attitudes and actions, which, in human terms, are impossible to change. Too little is said for the dimension of prayer in repairing these unhappy relationships. Christian counselors and pastors, if they are going to minister effectively, must operate in this second dimension, depending upon the Holy Spirit for supernatural discernment and wisdom.

Third, care and creativity must be used in restoring divorced (and sometimes remarried) persons to the church. This means loving and accepting people where they are in their spiritual experience and encouraging them to grow in Christ. For some this may involve submitting to the care and discipline of the church to restore them to fellowship and service. Too often the focus has been on the psychological and emotional recovery from divorce, with little emphasis on people's spiritual needs for forgiveness and restoration to Christ's church.

For too long we have tolerated a growing underworld of persons displaced from Christian fellowship due to divorce and remarriage. It is time to find ways to restore such persons to the church without destroying our standards of marital fidelity and ethics in human relationships.

Divorced persons need to experience reconciliation with the Lord and with his people (especially those divorced on unbiblical grounds). They desperately need to return home to the Father's house. We, in turn, need to be ready to welcome them back from the far country with the same love and compassion God has shown us. There is no place for the attitude of the elder brother in the story of the Prodigal Son. We as Christians still believe in a waiting Father who welcomes prodigals home. Above all, we need to share the Father's heart with those estranged from the family of God. This love is captured best in a poem by Bob Benson:

> And I was thinking about God
> He sure has plenty of children
>> plenty of artists
>> plenty of singers
>> and carpenters
> and candlestick makers
>> and preachers
>> and plenty of everybody . . .
>> except you.
> And there will always be
> an empty spot in His heart—
> and a vacant chair at His table
> when you're not home.[1]

If we can capture the gracious spirit of God's heart in these lines, it will be easy to answer the question, "Is there life after divorce?" with a resounding "Yes!" Is it a tearless, conflict-free life? No! It involves a real spirit of compassion and love by Christian counselors, congregations, and pastors to restore those whose marriages have died. And it requires a sense of humility and repentance on the part of those who have been divorced.

If both of these conditions are met, we can celebrate the return of lost sons and daughters to the Father's house. May we capture the spirit of God's heart on this matter. Then the end of this writing will not be an end, but a new beginning for many.

APPENDIX 1

HELPFUL BOOKS FOR COUNSELING THE DIVORCED AND THE DIVORCING

Adams, Jay E., *Marriage, Divorce and Remarriage in the Bible* (Grand Rapids: Zondervan Publishing House, 1980). This is an excellent review of a Reformation understanding of divorce and remarriage.

Bouma, Mary LaGrand, *Divorce in the Parsonage* (Minneapolis: Bethany House Publishers, 1979). Written by a pastor's wife, this deals with the pastor's marriage and the problem of divorce in the parsonage. Some very practical tips are included to enrich pastors' and seminarians' marriages.

Duty, Guy, *Divorce and Remarriage* (Minneapolis: Bethany House Publishers, 1967). Duty argues for the innocent party's right to remarry.

Fisher, Bruce, *Rebuilding: When Your Relationship Ends* (San Luis Obispo, Calif.: Impact Publishers, 1981). This book outlines the recovery process for people who have been divorced.

Foster, Richard J., *Money, Sex, and Power* (San Francisco: Harper and Row, Publishers, 1985). This is an excellent look at issues that destroy the American family, including a good section on marriage and divorce.

Heth, William A., and Wenham, Gordon J., *Jesus and Divorce* (Nashville: Thomas Nelson Publishers, 1984). This book describes the conservative, no divorce/no remarriage position based upon early church tradition.

Hosier, Helen Kooiman, *To Love Again: Remarriage for the Christian* (Nashville: Abingdon Press, 1985). The author stresses the efforts made to save a marriage that finally ended in divorce. This book endorses the concept of remarriage for Christians from the perspective of God's grace and forgiveness for past failures.

Klagsbrun, Francine, *Married People: Staying Together in the Age of Divorce* (New York: Bantam Books, 1985). This book contains a helpful description of what keeps marriages intact and what causes them to disintegrate.

Laney, J. Carl, *A Guide to Church Discipline* (Minneapolis: Bethany House Publishers, 1985). This book discusses the steps of church discipline to restore members to fellowship following divorce.

Laney, J. Carl, *The Divorce Myth* (Minneapolis: Bethany House Publishers, 1981). This is a textual study of Scripture as it relates to divorce. Basically, the author opposes remarriage following divorce.

Pearson, Bob and Kathy, *Single Again: Remarrying for the Right Reasons* (Ventura, Calif.: Regal Books, 1985). The authors construct a guide for remarried couples, stressing the importance of making the second marriage a success.

Rambo, Lewis R., *The Divorcing Christian* (Nashville: Abingdon Press, 1983). The author goes through the issues confronting Christians who get divorced.

Richards, Larry, *Remarriage: A Healing Gift from God* (Waco, Tex.: Word Books, 1981). This book emphasizes a hermeneutic of grace as it applies to the divorce and remarriage issue.

Small, Dwight Hervey, *Remarriage and God's Renewing Grace* (Grand Rapids: Baker Book House, 1986). The author outlines a position favoring remarriage, based upon a dispensational method of biblical interpretation.

Smith, Harold Ivan, *I Wish Someone Understood My Divorce* (Minneapolis: Augsburg Publishing House, 1986). A helpful guide, from the perspective of someone who has experienced the pain of parting.

Steele, Paul E., and Ryrie, Charles C., *Meant to Last: A Christian View of Marriage, Divorce, and Remarriage* (Wheaton, Ill.: Victor Books, 1983). The authors address leadership concerns in the church and argue for limited use of divorced and remarried people in the church as secretaries, choir members, and phone callers. They discourage the return to the roles of pastor and/or missionary for persons who have been divorced and remarried.

Thompson, David A., *Recovering From Divorce* (Minneapolis: Bethany House Publishers, 1982). A workbook for pastors.

Towner, Jason, *Jason Loves Jane, But They Got a Divorce* (Nashville: Impact Books, 1978). A very personal book that helps the reader feel the emotional dimension of divorce, this tells the story of the author's own divorce.

APPENDIX 2

DIVORCE RECOVERY GROUP PROGRAM

Group Leader's Guide

This section is designed to be used by a group leader to stimulate and direct positive discussion. The leader should be assisted by one other person who can help clarify issues for the leader and the participants. It is further suggested that it be a "closed group," that is, allowing no new members into the group once the process is started. This will assist in creating a confidential environment, conducive to sharing at a deeper level than otherwise possible in an "open group." The program could be modular, running quarterly or semi-annually (as people express interest), with an on-going care/support group being made available once the structured group-counseling process is completed.

Time should not be an intimidating factor. Some sections will need more attention than others, depending on the needs of the group. Leaders should be sensitive to this issue and pace the process accordingly. Ideally the program should be covered in one and one-half to two hours per week over a period of six to eight weeks. It can also be structured into a two-day weekend retreat.

The questions are designed to avoid yes/no or short answers, so as to elicit the greatest possible response. The questions listed are merely suggestive, and additional questions may be added by the leader.

SECTION I—WHO ARE YOU?

1. Describe your childhood (ages 1–18). What significant events influenced your life positively and negatively during this time?
2. Describe your parents. What were they like? In what ways did they influence your life positively and negatively?
3. Describe the ways your parents related to each other. In what ways did they show their love and express their anger toward one another?
4. Describe yourself in terms of positive and negative traits. In what ways do you think you will be remembered when you are gone?
5. Describe your past values. What has been important to you?
6. Describe your past goals. Which ones have been achieved/not achieved?
7. Describe the most significant experience in your life.
8. Who has had the greatest impact on your life? Describe in what ways that person has affected you.
9. Describe your past social life. What kinds of influence (positive/negative) have your friends had on your life?
10. Describe your spiritual life to date. What has happened in your relationship to God and how has that affected you and those around you?

SECTION II—WHERE HAVE YOU BEEN?

1. Describe your courtship with your former spouse. What attracted you to him/her? What interests did you share? What made you finally decide to get married?
2. Describe your former spouse in terms of positive/negative character traits.
3. Describe your expectations regarding your marriage before going to the altar. What do you think were your spouse's expectations?
4. Describe your first year of marriage. What were your successes and what were your disappointments?
5. What goals and values did you share/not share?
6. When and in what ways did you sense trouble in your marriage? What did you do, or not do, to rescue the relationship?
7. Describe ways that you believe you contributed to the breakdown of your relationship. In what ways do you feel your former spouse contributed to the breakup?
8. What were your feelings about getting a divorce?
9. Describe how your divorce affected your life in terms of relationships with relatives, friends and children.
10. Describe how your divorce has affected you in the following ways (address one at a time): emotionally, socially, economically and spiritually.
11. Describe personal traits that you feel make you lovable and worth knowing as a person.

SECTION III—WHAT ARE YOU THINKING AND FEELING?

1. In what ways are you dealing with your anger and guilt resulting from your divorce?
2. Describe your present feelings about your divorce. Where do you place yourself in the grieving process?
3. Describe your feelings about asking for and offering forgiveness for past actions.
4. Describe how you have handled the judgment of others as a result of your divorce.
5. What lessons did you learn from your divorce (particularly, what did you learn about yourself)?

6. What are some of the positive memories of your past relationship?
7. What are you doing to "unpack" mentally from your journey through divorce and to "get on with your life"?
8. What *can* be changed that needs to be changed in your life? What *cannot* be changed right now?
9. Describe the anxieties present in your life right now. In what ways can these be eliminated by personal effort?
10. Describe ways in which you believe God is working things out for good in your life.

SECTION IV—WHAT ARE YOU DOING?

1. Describe your social life, positively and negatively.
2. What are you doing to rehabilitate yourself (self-improvement programs, schooling, travel)? What is this doing to make you feel good about yourself?
3. Describe how your divorce has affected your employment (job performance/potential). How have you dealt with the conflict between family responsibilities and the demands of your work?
4. In what ways are you a different person since your divorce? How does this perception affect the way you feel and act?
5. What are you doing in the *present* to make your *future* bright?
6. Describe your positive and negative feelings about being a single person.
7. Describe what you see as the biggest obstruction for emotional/spiritual growth in your life. What are you doing about it?
8. Describe how you have dealt with the link in the Bible between divorce and moral failure. What kind of difficulties have you encountered in attempting to confess and repent of spiritually destructive attitudes and actions?
9. Describe your relationship with your children. In what ways has your divorce affected your relationship with your children?
10. Describe the major adjustments you have had to make in becoming a single parent or a separated parent. What

have you done to maintain a good relationship with your children?

SECTION V—WHERE ARE YOU GOING?

1. Describe what you would like to accomplish in the following areas in the next five years: vocational, financial, social, emotional, and spiritual.
2. Describe steps you are taking in the following areas to make your dreams a reality: vocational, financial, social, emotional, and spiritual.
3. Describe how you will reconstruct your spiritual life, in terms of *worship, witness,* and *service.*
4. Describe ways you can change your *thinking* and *feeling* about yourself and others.
5. Describe ways you can reconstruct your social life, in terms of *terminating* some relationships, *maintaining* present relationships, and *starting* new relationships.
6. Describe your dreams for your children. What are you doing to make these dreams reality?
7. Describe ways in which you will love yourself, love others, and love God.
8. Describe what you are going to do to forsake destructive past attitudes and actions toward *yourself, others,* and *God.*
9. Describe what goals you have selected to help you grow *personally, socially,* and *spiritually.*

NOTES

Chapter 1. The Causes of Divorce

1. Charles R. Swindoll, *Come Before Winter and Share My Hope* (Wheaton, Ill.: Tyndale House Publishers, 1985), 31.
2. Allan Bloom, *The Closing of the American Mind* (New York: Simon and Schuster, Inc., 1987), 25.
3. Ibid., 57.
4. Edward R. Dayton, *What Ever Happened to Commitment?* (Grand Rapids: Zondervan Publishing House, 1984), 35.
5. Ibid., 70.
6. James C. Dobson, *Straight Talk to Men and Their Wives* (Waco, Tex.: Word, 1980), 102.
7. Francine Klagsbrun, *Married People: Staying Together in the Age of Divorce* (New York: Bantam Books, 1985), 79.
8. Ibid., 16.
9. Ibid., 14.
10. Dayton, *What Ever Happened to Commitment?*, 16.
11. Os Guinness, *In Two Minds* (Downers Grove, Ill.: InterVarsity Press, 1976), 97.
12. William E. Hulme, *The Pastoral Care of Families* (Nashville: Abingdon Press, 1962), 68.
13. Jason Towner, *Jason Loves Jane, But They Got a Divorce* (Nashville: Impact Books, 1978), 12.

189

Chapter 2. The Crisis of Divorce

1. "Jesus replied, 'Moses permitted you to divorce your wives because your hearts were hard. But it was not this way from the beginning. I tell you that anyone who divorces his wife except for marital unfaithfulness, and marries another woman, commits adultery'" (Matt. 19:8–9 NIV).

2. "But if the unbeliever leaves, let him do so. A believing man or woman is not bound in such circumstances; God has called us to live in peace" (1 Cor. 7:15 NIV).

3. Jay Adams, Guy Duty and Dwight Small argue for the legitimacy of remarriage following divorce based upon the exception clauses of Matthew 19:9 and 1 Corinthians 7:15. J. Carl Laney and Heth-Wenham argue against remarriage based upon these passages. (See Bibliography for suggestions for further reading.)

4. "Haven't you read," he [Jesus] replied, "that at the beginning the Creator made them male and female, and he said: 'For this reason a man will leave his father and mother and be united to his wife, and the two will become one flesh?' So they are no longer two, but one. Therefore, what God has joined together, let not man separate" (Matt. 19:4–6 NIV).

5. "Wife of your marriage covenant" is taken from Malachi 2:14–15, where God speaks of the *primary evil of divorce* as having "broken faith with her, though she is your partner, the wife of your marriage covenant . . . so guard yourself and your spirit, and do not break faith with the wife of your youth."

6. "One Million Statistics Paint Portrait of Who We Are," *USA Today*, 1–3 April 1988.

7. Mary LaGrand Bouma, *Divorce in the Parsonage* (Minneapolis: Bethany House Publishers, 1979), 12.

8. Douglas A. Anderson, *New Approaches to Family Pastoral Care*, part of the Creative Pastoral Care and Counseling Series, ed. Howard J. Clinebell, Jr. (Philadelphia: Fortress Press, 1980), 81.

9. J. Carl Laney, *A Guide to Church Discipline* (Minneapolis: Bethany House Publishers, 1985), 69.

10. Wayne E. Oates, *Pastoral Care and Counseling in Grief and Separation*, part of the Creative Pastoral Care and Counseling Series, ed. Howard J. Clinebell, Jr. (Philadelphia: Fortress Press, 1976), 6–7.

11. Ibid., 30.

12. Ibid., 7.

13. Joyce Landorf Heatherley, *Unworld People* (San Francisco: Harper and Row, 1987), 170.

14. This is the title of a book by Eugene H. Peterson, *A Long Obedience in the Same Direction* (Downers Grove, Ill.: InterVarsity Press, 1980).

15. M. Scott Peck, *People of the Lie: The Hope for Healing Human Evil* (New York: Simon and Schuster, 1983), 182–211.

Chapter 3. The Criticisms of Divorce

1. Deuteronomy 22:19 speaks of the consequences of marrying a virgin and then declaring she was not a virgin, when, in fact, she was. The price of such slander is a fine of money to the woman and an injunction against the man not to divorce her as long as he lives. Deuteronomy 22:29 speaks of a young man raping a virgin and being forced to marry her and never divorcing her. Deuteronomy 24:1–4 speaks of a woman who is divorced by her husband, is married to another man, and then is divorced from him. The reference warns that her first husband must not remarry her.

2. This exclusion clause "except for unfaithfulness" is accepted by most scholars as biblical grounds for divorce. This right, however, doesn't have to be acted upon. The spouse can offer forgiveness instead.

3. William A. Heth and Gordon J. Wenham, *Jesus and Divorce* (Nashville: Thomas Nelson Publishers, 1984), 19–44.

4. Ibid., 73–99.

5. Ibid., 151.

6. Ibid., 200.

7. G. Bromiley, *God and Marriage* (Grand Rapids: Eerdmans Publishing Company, 1980), 40–41.

8. Heth and Wenham, *Jesus and Divorce*, 79–80.

9. Guy Duty, *Divorce and Remarriage* (Minneapolis: Bethany House Publishers, 1967), 127–128.

10. For a good understanding of the feelings of failure endured by a Christian getting a divorce, read Jason Towner's *Jason Loves Jane, But They Got a Divorce* (Nashville: Impact Books, 1978).

11. Romans 1:18–32 portrays a man's downhill slide into depravity and sexual unfaithfulness.

12. Mark R. McMinn and James D. Foster, "The Mind Doctors," *Christianity Today*, Vol. 33, No. 6 (8 April 1988), 16–20.

13. Dwight Hervey Small, *Remarriage and God's Renewing Grace* (Grand Rapids: Baker Book House, 1986), 50–51.

14. Ibid., 58.

15. James C. Dobson, *Straight Talk to Men and Their Wives*, 92.

16. Towner, *Jason Loves Jane, But They Got a Divorce*, 54.

17. Jay E. Adams, *Marriage, Divorce, and Remarriage in the Bible* (Grand Rapids: Zondervan Publishing House, 1980), 24–25.

18. Wayne E. Oates, *Pastoral Care and Counseling in Grief and Separation*, part of the Creative Pastoral Care and Counseling Series, ed. Howard J. Clinebell, Jr. (Philadelphia: Fortress Press, 1976), 75–76.

19. Small, *Remarriage and God's Renewing Grace*, 193–194.

Chapter 4. Some Pictures of Divorce

1. Dobson, *Straight Talk to Men and Their Wives*, 92.

2. LaGrand Bouma, *Divorce in the Parsonage*, 11.

3. Towner, *Jason Loves Jane, But They Got a Divorce*, 91.

4. Dobson, *Straight Talk to Men and Their Wives*, 178.

5. LaGrand Bouma, *Divorce in the Parsonage*, 59.

6. Dobson, *Straight Talk to Men and Their Wives*, 108–109.

7. Ibid., 109.

8. Ibid., 93–94.

9. Ibid., 100.

10. Lewis B. Smedes, *Caring and Commitment: Learning to Live the Love We Promise* (San Francisco: Harper and Row, Publishers, 1988), 77.

11. Ibid.

12. Ibid., 120.

Chapter 5. The Process of Divorce

1. Paul Bohannan, "The Six Stations of Divorce," in *Divorce and After*, ed. Paul Bohannan (New York: Doubleday and Company, 1970), 33–34.

2. C. S. Lewis, *Mere Christianity* (New York: The Macmillan Company, 1958), 82.

3. Bruce Fisher, *Rebuilding: When Your Relationship Ends* (San Luis Obispo, Calif.: Impact Publishers, 1981), 1.

4. Ibid., 2.

5. The exception is two books which are written by Christians and designed to help people walk through the divorce process: Jim Smoke, *Growing Through Divorce* (Eugene, Ore.: Harvest House Publishers, 1976) and Richard P. Olson and Carole Della Pia-Terry, *Help for Remarried Couples and Families* (Valley Forge, Penn.: Judson Press, 1984).

6. Landorf Heatherley, *Unworld People*, 210.

7. Fisher, *Rebuilding: When Your Relationship Ends*, 9.

8. Bohannan, *Divorce and After*, 37.

9. Abigail Trafford, *Crazy Time: Surviving Divorce* (New York: Bantam Books, 1982), 99–100.

10. Olson and Pia-Terry, *Help for Remarried Couples and Families*, 81–82.

11. See LaGrand Bouma's *Divorce in the Parsonage* for a general portrait of the effects of divorce on pastors and their wives.

12. David A. Thompson, *Recovering From Divorce* (Minneapolis: Bethany House Publishers, 1982).

13. Smoke, *Growing Through Divorce*, 80.

14. Towner, *Jason Loves Jane, But They Got a Divorce*, 169.

Chapter 6. The Person Who Intervenes

1. Richard J. Foster, *Money, Sex, and Power* (San Francisco: Harper and Row, 1985), 235–236.

2. Ibid., 236.

3. Henry Crady Davis, *Design for Preaching* (Philadelphia: Fortress Press, 1958), 133–134.

4. John R. W. Stott, *Between Two Worlds: The Art of Preaching in the Twentieth Century* (Grand Rapids: Eerdmans Publishing Company, 1982), 268.

5. Edward F. Markquart, *Quest for Better Preaching* (Minneapolis: Augsburg Publishing House, 1985), 118.

6. Oates, *Pastoral Care and Counseling in Grief and Separation*, 25.

7. Towner, *Jason Loves Jane, But They Got a Divorce*, 44.

8. Howard J. Clinebell, Jr., *Growth Counseling for Marriage Enrichment*, part of the Creative Pastoral Care and Counseling Series, ed. Howard J. Clinebell, Jr. (Philadelphia: Fortress Press, 1976), 68–69.

9. Smedes, *Caring and Commitment: Learning to Live the Love We Promise*, 112.

10. Ibid., 114.

11. Howard W. Stone, *Using Behavioral Methods in Pastoral Counseling*, part of the Creative Pastoral Care and Counseling Series, ed. Howard J. Clinebell, Jr. (Philadelphia: Fortress Press, 1980), 36.

12. Lawrence M. Brammer, *The Helping Relationship: Process and Skills* (Englewood Cliffs, N.J.: Simon and Schuster, 1988), 51–52.

13. Klagsbrun, *Married People: Staying Together in the Age of Divorce*, 289.

14. Ibid., 291–292.

Chapter 7. The Context of Divorce

1. Bloom, *The Closing of the American Mind*, 118.

2. Ibid., 119.

3. The early believers "devoted themselves to the apostles' teaching and to fellowship, to the breaking of bread and to prayer" (Acts 2:42 NIV). Early believers were known for their close fellowship with one another.

4. Towner, *Jason Loves Jane, But They Got a Divorce*, 119.

5. Dayton, *What Ever Happened to Commitment?*, 80.

6. Gary R. Collins, *Innovative Approaches to Counseling*, part of the Resources for Christian Counseling Series, ed. Gary R. Collins (Waco, Tex.: Word Books, Publishers, 1986), 30.

7. Laney, *A Guide to Church Discipline*, 35.

8. Ibid., 126.

9. M. Scott Peck, *The Different Drum—Community Making and Peace* (New York: Simon and Schuster, 1987), 61.

10. C. S. Lewis, *Mere Christianity* (New York: The Macmillan Company, 1958), 83–84.

11. Craig Dykstra, "Family Promises," in *Faith and Families*, ed. Lindell Sawyers (Philadelphia: The Geneva Press, 1986), 137.

12. Ibid., 138.

13. Ibid., 142–143.

14. Sheldon Vanauken, *Under the Mercy* (Nashville: Thomas Nelson Publishers, 1985), 147–148.

15. Dykstra, "Faith Promises," in *Faith and Families*, 152–153.

16. Towner, *Jason Loves Jane, But They Got a Divorce*, 137.

17. Ibid., 41–42.

18. Ibid., 143.

Chapter 8. The Challenge of Remarriage

1. Charles R. Swindoll, *Strike the Original Match* (Portland, Ore.: Multnomah Press, 1980), 165.
2. Trafford, *Crazy Time: Surviving Divorce*, 179.
3. Ibid., 180.
4. Towner, *Jason Loves Jane, But They Got a Divorce*, 126.
5. Olson and Pia-Terry, *Help for Remarried Couples and Families*, 42.
6. Dobson, *Straight Talk to Men and Their Wives*, 121.
7. Sally Squires, "All in the Stepfamily," *The Seattle Times*, 17 December 1987, E1.
8. Emily and John Visher, *Stepfamilies* (New York: Brunner/Mazel, Publishers, 1979), 48.
9. Squires.
10. Ibid.
11. Elizabeth A. Carter and Monica McGoldrick, *The Family Life Cycle: A Framework for Family Therapy* (New York: Garnder Press, 1980), 268.
12. Ibid., 269–270.
13. Carter and McGoldrick, 274–275.
14. Squires.
15. Ibid.

Chapter 9. Divorce and the Seasons of Life

1. This whole book of the Old Testament Scriptures struggles with the passage of time and the problem of meaning. The writer's conclusion is that life "under the sun" is meaningless apart from God. It is an excellent book to read and reread to get a grasp of how modern man apart from God feels about life.
2. Gail Sheehy, *Passages* (New York: Bantam Books, 1974) and *Pathfinders* (New York: William Morrow and Co., 1981). Both books deal with predictable crises in the adult life cycle. *Passages* expands upon Daniel Levinson's study of adult life cycles of men that later was published as *The Seasons of a Man's Life*. Sheehy's study included a broader age/sex spectrum than Levinson, including women, young adults (18 to 30), and the elderly (50 to 65+). *Pathfinders* primarily deals with a study of "risk takers" who lead the way for others into various seasons of life.

3. Daniel J. Levinson, *The Seasons of a Man's Life* (New York: Ballatine Books, 1978). His studies at Yale were the basis for numerous contemporary studies in life-cycle issues.

4. Erikson's view of the life cycle is described in the following: *Childhood and Society* (New York: W. W. Norton, 1950) and "Identity and the Life Cycle," *Psychological Issues* 1 (1959): 1–171.

5. Levinson, 57–62.

6. Naomi Golan, *Passing Through Transitions* (New York: The Free Press, 1981), 47.

7. Levinson, 141.

8. Ibid., 140.

9. Florence W. Kaslow and Richard I. Ridenour, *The Military Family* (New York: The Guilford Press, 1984), 151.

10. Sheehy, *Passages*, 300.

11. Ibid., 301.

12. Ibid., 215.

13. Levinson, 192.

14. Gary R. Collins, *Christian Counseling: A Comprehensive Guide, revised edition* (Dallas: Word, 1988), 203.

15. Levinson, 257.

16. Paul Tournier, *A Place For You* (New York: Harper and Row, 1968), 162.

17. Jerry and Mary White, *The Christian in Mid-Life* (Colorado Springs: NavPress, 1980), 158.

18. Lillian B. Rubin, *Intimate Strangers: Men and Women Together* (New York: Harper and Row, 1983), 67.

Chapter 10. Divorce and the Ministry

1. Leadership Forum, "When the Pastor Gets a Divorce," *Leadership* 3 (Fall, 1981): 119.

2. Ibid.

3. Edward B. Bratcher, *The Walk-on-Water Syndrome* (Waco, Tex.: Word, 1984), 24.

4. Ibid.

5. David and Vera Mace, *What's Happening to Clergy Marriages?* (Nashville: Abingdon, 1980), 32, 40–41. A study was made of 166 clergymen and 155 wives. A survey was distributed to the participants requesting they list areas of need for family enrichment and list areas where wives need help to adjust to their husband's ministry. A

third questionnaire was given the participants asking them to list advantages and disadvantages of clergy marriage.

6. Gordon McDonald, "The Private Times of the Public Minister," *Leadership* 3 (Fall, 1981): 102–04.

7. Roger C. Palms, "Four Keys to Better Family Life," *Leadership* 3 (Fall, 1981): 40.

8. This is discussed in an excellent volume by Kent and Barbara Hughes, *Liberating Ministry from the Success Syndrome* (Wheaton, Ill.: Tyndale House, 1988). See also Louis McBurney's volume in the Resources for Christian Counseling series, *Counseling Christian Workers* (Waco, Tex.: Word, 1986).

9. Christina Maslach, *Burnout—The Cost of Caring* (Englewood Cliffs, N. J.: Prentice-Hall, 1982), 90–107.

10. Gordon McDonald, *Restoring Your Spiritual Passion* (Nashville: Oliver-Nelson, 1986), 160.

Epilogue

1. Towner, *Jason Loves Jane, But They Got a Divorce,* 78.

INDEX

David A. Thompson

David A. Thompson is professor of practical theology and counseling at Bethany College of Missions in Bloomington, Minnesota. He has been a pastor, hospital chaplain, college teacher, and chaplain in the U.S. Navy during eighteen years of ministry.

He received a B.S. degree from the University of Wisconsin (Superior); attended Trinity Evangelical Divinity School and the Lutheran Brethren Seminary, graduating from the latter with a M.Div. degree; received the M.S.E. in Counseling from the University of Wisconsin (Oshkosh); and presently is a Ed.D. Candidate in Christian Education at Trinity Evangelical Divinity School. He is an ordained minister in the Free Methodist Church of North America. David and his wife Judy are the parents of three teenage boys.

The author has written three counseling workbooks for pastors and counselors: *A Premarital Guide for Couples and Their Counselors, Five Steps Toward a Better Marriage,* and *Recovering from Divorce.*